The Prodigal Couple:

Our Extraordinary Experience with God's Extravagant Grace

By

Eric & Wendy Darline Ingram

The Prodigal Couple Copyright © 2017 by Eric Ingram & Wendy Darline Ingram.

All rights reserved. No part of this book may be reproduced in any form without permission in writing from the author.

Eric Ingram & Wendy Darline Ingram

Visit our website at www.prodigalcouple.com

Printed in the United States of America

First Printing: Oct 2017

ISBN-13: 978-0-692-97497-1

ISBN-10: 0692974970

100 Fold Life Publishing

~*DEDICATION*~

To God

God told us both separately that we were soul mates, but our flesh was weak. We gave into our own selfish needs and wants, leaving God out. So, we ended up hurting each other and sabotaging God's plan for our lives. We moved on and tried to make do with the new lives we chose. But God....

Once you have tasted and seen his best for you, nothing and no one else will do. It just never compared to what God had shown us. So, when we separately came to the end of ourselves and surrendered to God, God was able to pick up those broken pieces and turn it into his greatest masterpiece.

Because God is faithful to complete that which *He Has Started*. When God is for you, nothing can be against you, not even yourself. We let counterfeit love, hurt and distractions and egos get in the way of God's perfect love affair. We don't want to let that happen to you.

~BLURBS~

My wife and I met Wendy Darline in Maui 16 years ago, and we have found her to be an amazing and wonderful person. She was involved in our ministry for 15 years, an ordained minister and a family friend. One thing that always stands out about Wendy is that she is a fighter and more than an overcomer. Another is she really cares about people and is always helpful, encouraging, empowering and does all she can to help in every way possible. It has been a privilege to know Pastor Wendy, and we have found her to be a person of great integrity.

    Pastor Earl and Jana Thurner, Desire Of All Nations Ministry

I just wanted you to know that having you as a friend has healed parts of me that forgot to go out and play, dance and laugh. Maybe forgot isn't the right word, I think the words are I was too afraid to. These things that happen to us in life, either chip away at us or build us up. Either way, you have made me feel safe to come out and play, rise up and claim my happiness!

    Jill Schenkel

In October of 2016, Wendy was sitting in my living room and had just experienced a minor stroke from the tumor on your pituitary gland. A righteous anger swelled up within me - *You Will Live And Not Die*! You will live to tell of his goodness and faithfulness! Your healing will glorify him! After that, the word '*Acceleration*' came into my mind: accelerated healing, accelerated restoration, accelerated blessing - "exceedingly and abundantly above all you could ask or think!" Ever since then, God has been accelerating the manifestation of his promises over you. I praise him for his great and mighty victory in your life... now thanks be unto God who always causes us to Triumph in Christ! You are his beloved!

    Noelle Wylie

~*PREFACE*~

"Every good and perfect gift comes from the father." Jms 1:17

... However, it may not look good to us at the time. How many times have you volunteered at church or started a bible study or did something you felt was "of God?" It may have been God-inspired, but did God actually say, "Do this now?"

"Every good thing is not a God thing." Helen Ingram

I was so convinced that this is what I should be doing to move forward, that I just went into "Pastor" mode. I was so used to having a church, a ministry, and a cell group. My heart was just so full of gratitude to God for bringing me this seemingly perfect Man. That's not to be condescending; he was perfect for me. He was literally everything God told me he would be, plus beautiful to boot. It's okay to call a man beautiful, right? ;)

Well, he was, and my heart was so connected to his. We would complete each other's thoughts and hear from God simultaneously. It was crazy. When we both heard from God that we were who God had intended for each other, that was the German Chocolate icing on the proverbial cake. With all those confirmations, it just seemed logical to move at a rapid pace. It actually didn't feel rapid because of how long it took me to get there. It just seemed right to go all in. However, it was not God's perfect time. Nor was it for Eric and me. God's desires were bigger than ours, but we had to be stripped of ourselves before we could really grasp it all.

~TABLE OF CONTENTS~

~DEDICATION~ v

~BLURBS~ vi

~PREFACE~ vii

~TABLE OF CONTENTS~ ix

~INTRODUCTION~ xvii

    Eric: xvii

    Wendy: xxii

        ~The Parable of the Lost Son~ 1

~CHAPTER ONE~ 1

    The Year Before 1

    Wendy: God's Doing A New Thang! 1

    Eric: Who's Your Daddy? 3

~CHAPTER TWO~ 7

    The Divine Appointment! 7

    Wendy: His Gift Will Keep On Giving 7

    Eric: Get Oouutt! 12

~CHAPTER THREE~ 17

    The Waiting Game 17

Wendy: The Dating Game 17

Eric: You're Still Here?? 20

~CHAPTER FOUR~ 23

The Chance Encounter 23

Wendy: The Set up 23

Eric: Divine Encounter Of The God Kind 27

~CHAPTER FIVE~ 33

Three-Day Honeymoon 33

Wendy: It Is Him 33

Eric: Southern Hospitality 37

~CHAPTER SIX~ 41

The Calling 41

Wendy: Yes Lord 41

Eric: Wake Up It's Me, God 45

~CHAPTER SEVEN~ 51

Coming Up For Heir 51

Wendy: Everything Was Falling Into Place 51

Eric: Drop That Bible-Base 52

~CHAPTER EIGHT~ 55

Acceleration! 55

Eric: Let The Healing Begin 55

Wendy: Serving God 58

~CHAPTER NINE~ 61

    Redding Is Calling 61

    Wendy: Denied Tres Times 61

    Eric: Shaken & Stirred 63

    Wendy: Jilted 65

~CHAPTER TEN~ 69

    On Fire For God!! 69

    Eric: Stripped To The Bone 69

~CHAPTER ELEVEN~ 73

    In God We Trust 73

    Wendy: The Rug Got Pulled Out 73

~CHAPTER TWELVE~ 81

    Serving God No Matter What 81

    Eric: Breath, Wind & Fire 81

    Wendy: About My Father's Business 83

~CHAPTER THIRTEEN~ 87

    The Day Of Reckoning 87

    Eric: Time to Pay The Piper 87

    Wendy: Betrayed And Scared 90

~CHAPTER FOURTEEN~ 97

Heart Breaker 97
Eric: The Painful Revelation...................................... 97

~CHAPTER FIFTEEN~ 105
The Walking Dead 105
Eric: Roaming The Desert 105
Wendy: Hardened Heart 107

~CHAPTER SIXTEEN~ 115
Free At Last.. 115
Eric: Jesus Take The Wheel!................................... 115

~CHAPTER SEVENTEEN~ 121
Picking Up The Pieces.. 121
Wendy: Repentance Is Key..................................... 121
Eric: Checking In.. 124

~CHAPTER EIGHTEEN~ 127
Dying In The Wilderness 127
Wendy: Trusting My Process And God................. 127
Eric: The Suddenly Of God..................................... 130

~CHAPTER NINETEEN~ 139
Pressing In For The Truth 139
Wendy: God Confirms A Second Time................. 139

~CHAPTER TWENTY~ 149

The Circle Of Life 149

Eric: My Fathers In Heaven 149

~CHAPTER TWENTY-ONE~ 157

Friends Helping Friends 157

Wendy: Revelation In A Storm 157

Eric: My Fathers' Favorite 159

~CHAPTER TWENTY-TWO~ 169

Year Of Restoration 169

Wendy: It is On! 169

Eric: Holy Spirit, Help! 170

~CHAPTER TWENTY-THREE~ 179

The Lone Ranger Strikes Again! 179

Eric: Whoa Kemo-Sabe! 179

~CHAPTER TWENTY-FOUR~ 186

Back On Track 186

Wendy: Everything's Accelerated 186

Eric: The Lion Awakens 190

~CHAPTER TWENTY-FIVE~ 193

The Leap Of Faith 193

Wendy: God Said Go 193

Eric: What Happened In Vegas 197

~CHAPTER TWENTY-SIX~ 200

- Wedding The Bells! 200
- Wendy: Fo Real Fo Real 200
- Eric: Married & Blessed 201

~CHAPTER TWENTY-SEVEN~ 202

- Sex Is Great For The Soul 203
- The Holy Spirit to Eric & Wendy: Let Love Rein...203

~EPILOGUE~ 221

- Eric & Wendy: Final Words 221
- The Call To Salvation Prayer 225
- What Now? 229

~APPENDIX A~ 231

- Eric & Wendy's 8-Year Timeline 231
- Eric & Wendy's Marriage Bootcamp 232
- * Engagement/Preparation For Marriage: 232
- * Anchor Your Foundation In The Word 233
- * Newlywed/Separated/On The Verge Of Divorce: 234
- * More For Separated/Divorce Couples: 237
- * Reassess Your Issues & Forgive 237

~APPENDIX B~ 241

- Daily Devotional: 241

-- A Letter To Me From The Lord: 241

-- Prayer For Patience In God's Timing: 244

-- Prayer To Break The Lone Ranger Spirit Off Of You: 244

-- Prayer To Break Soul Ties: 245

-- Call To Salvation Prayer: 246

-- Call To Dedicate Your Marriage to God: 247

~INDEX~ 249

Romans 8: 249

Proverbs 31: 10b-31 The Wife of Noble Character: 252

Isaiah. 61: 254

Ruth 4:1-17: 255

1 Kings 19: 258

1 Sam 25: Death of Samuel (Abigail) 260

Luke 10:28-33 28: 266

Mt 25: 1-13: 266

1 Corinthians 7 (NKJV): 267

Prv 6:16-19: 270

Gen 22:1-19: 270

Eric & Wendy Darline Ingram

~*INTRODUCTION*~

His Grace

"Three times I pleaded with the Lord to take it away from me. But he said to me, "My grace is sufficient for you, for my power is made perfect in weakness. Therefore, I will boast all the more gladly about my weaknesses, so that Christ's power may rest on me." 2 Cor 12: 8-9 NIV

Eric:

Grace. Christians throw this word around like it's the new meme of the week. "I'm not perfect, but I'm under grace." "Thank God I'm under grace." "We're not under the law; we're under grace." Televangelists tell us, "Grace is the unmerited favor of God." Really? Unmerited? Hmm. Some will say it means God gives it freely for us because we're undeserving of it. 'We're sinners,' they say. Really? God said, "We were made in His image and likeness" (Gen 1:26). Paul said, "We are heirs of God and co-heirs with Christ" (Rom 8:17). David said we were "fearfully and wonderfully made" (Ps 139:14). If this is true, then I ask, why are we identifying with what our enemy calls us?

Jesus came to set me free. It is the 'father of lies' and the 'accuser of the brethren' who wants me to keep identifying with my old self. But I am a new creation. I sin, but God doesn't identify me by the mistakes I make. He calls me his beloved son, the apple of his eye, and most importantly, son. And this is where grace comes into my life through my Lord and Savior Jesus Christ. I am identified in Him now. God doesn't count my mistakes anymore. Isaiah 43:25, God says "I, even I, am he who blots out your transgressions, for my own sake, and remembers your sins no more." He remembers our sins no more!! So why are we calling ourselves 'sinners?' If we're calling ourselves sinners, then Jesus' work on the cross was for nothing. He came to set the captives free. We are free. Free to love. Free to laugh. Free to live a prosperous life. Free to fall in love and marry the spouse of your dreams. We are free to live a joyous life no matter what sins you committed. Jesus did that for us. (John 10:10) Jesus, who knew no sin, became sin for us, that we might become the righteousness of God in Him. (2 Cor 5:21) Sin is enmity towards God.

> *"You adulterous people, don't you know that friendship with the world means enmity against God? Therefore, anyone who chooses to be a friend of the world becomes an enemy of God."*
> *James 4:4*

A friend of the world becomes an enemy of God. I will never be an enemy of God. That would be like choosing to play for the Washington Senators who lose to the Harlem Globetrotters every game for the rest of eternity. Jesus wins every battle, every game, every contest. No thank you. I'd rather be on the winning team. And God has open tryouts every second of every day. Join God's team. Win for eternity. You won't be sorry. Back to this thing called grace. God is holy. He does not allow sin. So let's look at a few interesting definitions of Grace:

1.(in Christian belief) the free and unmerited favor of God, as manifested in the salvation of sinners and the bestowal of blessings, divinely given talent or blessing.
"the graces of the Holy Spirit."

There goes the unmerited favor definition that we have all come to know. Next,

2. the condition or fact of being favored by someone.
"he fell from grace because of drug use at the Olympics."
synonyms: favor, approval, approbation, acceptance, esteem, regard, respect

This definition backs up the previous one. A condition or fact of being favored by someone. That someone in our case is God. Okay, my spirit's still not satisfied. Number 3,

3. a period officially allowed for payment of a sum due or for compliance with a law or condition, especially an extended period granted as a special favor.
"another three days' grace."
synonyms: deferment, deferral, postponement, suspension, adjournment, delay, pause

This one speaks to my unsettled spirit: A period officially allowed for compliance with a law or condition. Has God given you a job or task to do and you keep putting it off due to fear, distractions and/or procrastination? Obedience is the law.

> "As in obeying the voice of the Lord? Behold, to obey is better than sacrifice, And to heed than the fat of rams" 1 Sam 15:22

Your procrastination equals disobedience. Disobedience is a sin.

> "But it shall come to pass, if you do not obey the voice of the Lord your God, to observe carefully all His commandments and His statutes which I command you today, that all these curses will come upon you and overtake you:" Deut 28:15

The wages of sin is death.

> "For the wages of sin is death, but the gift of God is eternal life in Christ Jesus our Lord." Rom 6:23

Instead of meting out the deserved punishment for disobedience (read the curses in Deut 28), the Lord patiently waits--but growing impatient--for us to complete the task he has ordained for us to complete from the beginning of days. Whatever God has put on your heart, please start doing it today. Do you know where that desire to start that new business, create that new machine and build that new homeless shelter that hounds your spirit every day emanates from? GOD.

> "Delight yourself also in the Lord, And He shall give you the desires of your heart. Commit your way to the Lord, Trust also in Him, And He shall bring it to pass." Ps 37:4-5

Many people think the above scripture means, "If I am a good person, He will give me the things that I want?" Wrong! It means diligently seek out the things of God, and while you're doing that, He will put His desires in your heart for you to fulfill them. Commit to doing this His way, and He will bring it to pass. What is it? The very desire he puts in your heart.

> *"So is my word that goes out from my mouth: It will not return to me empty, but will accomplish what I desire and achieve the purpose for which I sent it." Is 55:11*

For anyone who says they do not know their purpose, there's your template on how to find your purpose. Make the Lord your all and all, and he will give you His all and all.

This is where God and I intersected. I was doing things my own way. Then one fate-filled morning, he asked me to start doing things His way. For 7 years I disobeyed Him. 7 years! He held back the curses from my life until I willingly came into alignment and obedience with Him and His Word. And my life is 100x joyous than I could ever have imagined. I want the same for you. He wants that for his children. He yearns and cries for you every second you are away from Him. Go back to Him. Trust Him. Listen to Him. Believe in Him. Love Him. You won't regret it.

That's my hope in writing this book. It's to help those who are on the fence about giving up the reins to your life to God Almighty. Is it scary? Is it hard? Yes. Will there be tears, trials, and tribulations? Definitely. But take heart, Jesus has overcome the

world. He's on our side. And if you don't know it yet, we win. :)...
By the Grace of God.

Wendy:

"But to each one of us, grace has been given as Christ apportioned it." Eph 4:7

When I gave my heart to my Lord, Jesus Christ, I gave him every part of me. His grace was real and tangible to me. To go from being broken to being whole was amazing! All I wanted to do was please God, serve God, and lead others to Him.

I was great at serving. Though I was never a saint, I was madly in love with my creator, my savior, and the Holy Spirit. I took time to learn them; how they thought; how they felt. I know all three are God, but if he took the time to separate them and to show me their roles, then I wanted to take the time to learn them that way as well. As the years went on, we grew, well I grew in him. Serving the trinity became very much my heart, my soul, and my purpose.

God saved me. He healed me and taught me because I completely surrendered to Him. I embraced Him as if I was a child learning how to think, act, respond and love in every situation. Trust me; it's not all been a picnic. I knew what my life was like without God, so to me, there was no turning back. I learned to love God's children as if he were my husband and his children came into the marriage with him. I asked God to not only give me a heart for his children but to love them the way he did. God taught me that love was not just feelings or actions, but it was the very essence of HIM.

"Whoever does not LOVE does Not know God, BECAUSE GOD IS LOVE." 1 John 4:8

I lost my ability to be a victim or to be defensive. I truly try to put myself into the other person's shoes before responding. I was learning to be selfless and walk out 1 Corinthians 13: 4-8a:

(Paraphrased) "God is patient, kind, he does not envy, or brag. God is not arrogant or rude. He does not insist on his own way; he is not irritable or resentful. God does not rejoice at wrong doing but rejoices in the Truth (his truth, the word of God), God bears all things (through His son, Jesus Christ), he believes all things according to his word, he hopes in all things, endures all things. God Never Ends! Wow! What I did not realize was how the devil would use this against me: in marriage, the church and life. You know that expression, 'Hurting people hurt people?' So I had to learn not to take it all so personally.

This came into play the entire time I was with Eric. See, God showed me His heart for Eric right away so that I would see past any facade that he had. I had to always deal with his heart. I allowed God to use me as a human vessel to show Eric the real God, the incredible, magnanimous God who loves him and wants good things for him, not the Sunday church God

Grace has played a huge part in our journey. There's been hurt; there's been betrayal, and there's been frustration. But there has also been Love, Power, Forgiveness, and Grace with a whole lot of Mercy. We are two imperfect people who desired above everything else to know God, who Loved God and who God wanted to bless despite the past. But God.

I lived for God my whole adult life, but I still had not experienced true love from a man, and my faith wavered that I ever would. Eric lived most of his adult life as a "good person," but he was not fulfilling his calling. But God chose this union, and we chose HIS perfect will. But God.

He wanted to make something powerful and great. And He chose us... (tears streaming) It started out as a love affair, but since became a story of two people from two seemingly different worlds deciding to take a chance. We fell down but got back up to accomplish the impossible.

We are good people with great hearts who were doing okay by ourselves. Despite all of our mistakes, we discovered a new level of Grace, first from God, then from each other. I loved Eric from the first moment I met him. No, not a lust love, a true agape love. I walked out 1 Corinthians 13 with him as best as I could. I learned a lot about myself along the way. The biggest lesson: God's choice is always better than our own.

> *"For my thoughts are not your thoughts, neither are your ways my ways," declares the Lord"* Is 55:8

Don't get me wrong; there are a lot of great, amazing and good looking people out there, But God knows what you need. He knows how to make a concoction of love, boldness, and strength that will cause:

* Friction - iron sharpening iron (Prv 27:17)

* Tenderness - nurturing healing to dry bones (Ez 37:1-14)

* Intimacy - that will quench the fiery darts of the enemy. (Eph 6:16)

* Passion - that would bring healing, restoration, and devotion. (Jer 33:6)

Equally yoked means that both people are completely surrendered to Abba Father in order to fulfill their call and to further HIS Kingdom. God is into the details. He will never let you down. He is faithful even if you run away. For Eric and I, God literally stood still and let us go our own ways, but He stayed steadfast till we ran back into his arms. That's the kind of Love our God is! Why would I choose to move out of God's grace? Ever heard that expression, 'It's too good to be true." That's what scared Eric and I. This is too good to be true, and we both felt we weren't worthy of God's perfect mating.

When Eric and I parted ways, it was the first time in my walk with God that I got mad at him. I finally expected His goodness, His best, and I got hurt. I couldn't believe my God put me through this. He knew Eric; he knew where Eric was at. Well, God knew me, too. God used Eric and I to work on each other for His sake. God knew he could trust me with Eric's heart and he also knew Eric would protect mine. God knew what we didn't. He knew us better than we knew ourselves. He gave us the grace to fall and to pick ourselves up. To experience other things and decide that God's way is the best. But God.

In hindsight, I'm actually glad I did fall. Not only did I discover God's true grace again, I also discovered how lovable I am. And once I finally understood that, God brought Eric back into my life. Eric loves me for me, scars and all. He loves me to the point that I can be my whole true self with him. I now know what it is like to be loved by a man for me. Not a version of me, but the whole me.

As for Eric, he gets a best friend and a true helpmate. A Proverbs 31:10b woman: "A wife of noble character who can find? She is worth far more than rubies..." A partner that will go with him wherever God will use him. A partner to do life and ministry with. Eric was given the gift of a queen, a warrior, someone who God felt would be a great mother to Eric's disciples, stepmother to his daughter and always have his back. I counted the cost early on in my walk. I got beat up and battered over time and only saw my scars.

But in listening to Eric, I discovered he saw all these other qualities in me I never knew. The same qualities God saw in me. See, I struggle with affirming myself. I need to be affirmed. I have always known how much God loved me, but I struggled with really believing there was a man who could find me worthy to be loved. But God saw my faithfulness, endurance, and my character as a warrior, a woman, and a mate, and He said to Eric, "This one right here is who I choose for you because she's passed all her tests and will cause you and your ministry no harm." But God! He knows me. He knows Eric. He chose us!!

When you're in God, and you have chosen to be all in, it's just that, a choice. Eric counted the cost and told God, "I'm all in." God asked Eric to get on the plane; Eric got on the plane. Eric chose me, us, ministry, and life together. Eric chose God, and I am God's choice for Eric. But God!

Revelation:

Wow! That was powerful to write down. The Holy Spirit is literally bathing me in love as I write this. Tears are burning my cheeks. I just got this revelation deep in my soul! I trusted God again. I chose to walk away from my past. I chose to get in the car, go to Vegas, and marry Eric, whom I had not seen in 6.5 years. I chose God's promise for my life! My revelation in writing all this down is that in the last 7 years, Eric is and was truly my soulmate. His sacrifices have proven that. But God

~*The Parable of the Lost Son*~

Luke 15:11-32 NIV: Jesus continued, " "There was a man who had two sons. The younger one said to his father, 'Father, give me my share of the estate.' 'So he divided his property between them." "Not long after that, the younger son got together all he had, set off for a distant country and there squandered his wealth in wild living. After he had spent everything, there was a severe famine in that whole country, and he began to be in need. So he went and hired himself out to a citizen of that country, who sent him to his fields to feed pigs. He longed to fill his stomach with the pods that the pigs were eating, but no one gave him anything." "When he came to his senses, he said, 'How many of my father's hired servants have food to spare, and here I am starving to death! I will set out and go back to my father and say to him: Father, I have sinned against heaven and against you. I am no longer worthy to be called your son; make me like one of your hired servants.' 'So he got up and went to his father. "But while he was still a long way off, his father saw him and was filled with compassion for him; he ran to his son, threw his arms around him and kissed him. "The son said to him, 'Father, I have sinned against heaven and against you. I am no longer worthy to be called your son.' "But the father said to his servants, 'Quick! Bring the best robe and put it on him. Put a ring on his finger and sandals on his feet. Bring the fattened calf and kill it. Let's have a feast and celebrate. For this son of mine was dead and is alive again; he was lost and is found." So they began to celebrate. "'Meanwhile, the older son was in the field. When he came near the house, he heard music and dancing. So he called one of the servants and asked him what was going on. 'Your brother has come,' he replied, 'and your father has killed the fattened calf because he has him back safe and sound.' "The older brother became angry and refused to go in. So his father went out and pleaded with him. But he answered his father, 'Look! All these years I've been slaving for you and never disobeyed your orders. Yet you never gave me even a young goat so I could celebrate with my friends. But when this son of yours who has squandered your property with prostitutes comes home, you kill the fattened calf for him!' "'My son,' the father said, 'you are always with me, and everything I have is yours. But we had to celebrate and be glad, because this brother of yours was dead and is alive again; he was lost and is found.'"

~CHAPTER ONE~

The Year Before

Wendy: God's Doing A New Thang!

The year before had been such a very difficult year, but I was determined to move past it all and press in for the promise God gave me. "I am doing a new thing. Let everyone and everything from your past go." That's easier said than done when you've been a pastor for over 20 years, married for 23 years and have numerous responsibilities, But God... His ways are not my ways

As I laid in recovery from yet another surgery, I asked God,

"How will we do this new thing? What about my marriage; my ministry; my finances; and my health? By the time I got out of the hospital, my husband had quit his job, short sale'd my home, filed bankruptcy, and was now asking for a divorce {I need to say right here, I chose to forgive my ex-husband right then. I wanted to be better, not bitter. And as the father of my son, I pray that someday He will encounter God's grace for his life}. I lost my medical insurance in the middle of my cancer treatments. On top of that, my church rescinded my ordination because a) pastors can't get divorced, and b) I must have some unspoken sin to have all this happening to me.

"What are you going to be able to do with all of this?" I asked God. He said clear as day, "Wendy I plan on doing a brand new thing. Just rest. I've seen your pain and collected your tears. Job well done with this life. Time to do a brand new thing." God took away all my "what abouts" in the blink of an eye and gave me Isaiah 43:19:

> *"See I am doing a new thing! Now it springs up; do not perceive it? I am making a way in the wilderness and streams in the wasteland."*

That's exactly how I was feeling, like a wasteland. Left for dead. Every day was a battle to choose Life and to focus on God's word and his views of me, instead of those around me.

Eric: Who's Your Daddy?

"Children are a gift from the Lord; they are a reward from him."
Ps 127:3

March 27, 2008, There I was, sitting in the hospital holding my newborn daughter. So beautiful. So soft. So precious. So...me. What did I do deserve her? I had been very careful not to have children until I was ready. The nature of my career, a stand-up comedian, turned screenwriter, is one of instability. One week, you're too busy to think. The next, crickets. I didn't want to be the type of father who was never home due to the obligations of his career. That's what soured me on doing stand-up. You're always on the road until you make it big. Always. I wanted to raise my children and be a present father like my father was. Very present. And I wanted everything in place before I started having kids. But life said, "It's time." And so here she is.

Her dark brown eyes looked deep into mine, and we started having our first father/daughter conversation.

"Who are you?," she said in her sweet voice.

"I'm your father," I said.

"Was that your voice I heard in my mother's stomach?"

"Yep."

Then she asked the question that pierced my soul.

"Are you going to take care of me?"

Sccuurrtt! Think before you speak, Eric. You can't lie to your children. I was a struggling writer with no prospects on the horizon. I was living in a studio apartment in North Hollywood while working as a security/doorman at one of LA's swankiest celebrity nightclub/hotels. The money I made there was good enough for me because all I cared about was having a place to sleep, eat, and write during the day. I didn't have a bedroom, health insurance, savings or a 401k. Simply put, I didn't have a plan. Well, I had my plan, not a daughter plan.

As she gripped my thumb with her baby fingers, a rush of being the family protector surged through me. I brought her forehead to mine, (something we still do to this day), and as we gazed into each other's eyes, these words shot up from the pit of my very being...

"I got you. Daddy got you."

Unfortunately, Daddy didn't have her. I was going through life as a walking zombie who was hell-bent on making it in Hollywood. This is my destiny, I know it. I had come to LA from New York in 2003 where I was a burgeoning stand-up comedian. I use to work out with a lot of today's hottest comedians back in my New York City days, but I put away the comedy skills in LA and became a 24/7 writer who also did commercials. I was straight for me, not for my daughter.

Working at the celebrity club started to wear on me. I'm not a club guy. I love music, and I like to dance, but the club life was never for me. Watching people night in and night out, come in all beautiful and dressed to the nines, then leave so drunk, I'd have to carry them to their cars. That is not my idea of fun. Even all of the "benefits" of being a doorman never impressed me. I don't care to be hit on by anyone in that environment because they're only doing it to get inside the club. You'd be amazed or disgusted at some of the things I was offered to let people into the club. Let's just say I understood Sodom and Gomorrah in a whole new light. And Hollywood is next level.

Whenever a big entertainment event came to town: Grammies, Oscars, The Billboard Music Awards, The BET Awards or movie premieres, our hotel/nightclub was the hot spot. The more I worked these events; the more my spirit was dying inside.

Now at this time, I wasn't going to church, and I wasn't seeking God. I was just a good, law-abiding person. I was a good employee who did my job well. I've never drank nor smoked. I had morals, was fun-loving, respectful, gave money to the homeless. You know, a good person.

CALL TO ACTION:

Where were you in your life when you first realized the Lord was calling out to you or you had an inclination that things needed to change in your life?

_____

_____

_____

_____

_____

~CHAPTER TWO~

The Divine Appointment!

Wendy: His Gift Will Keep On Giving...

I woke up January 1st, 2009. God spoke to me so clearly, "Go to the beach. I want to spend time with you." I was so excited. God wants time with me! So, I got up that morning, grabbed my trusty bible and notebook, and headed to the beach. Looking forward to spending time with Him made me giddy like a schoolgirl as to what we had in store for me today. Never did I think it would be about a *new husband*, a new ministry, and a new life. So soon?!

When I was lying in the hospital bed, God gave me a choice: a) I can go home to be with Him (because I had done my job well) or b) I can go back so that he could give me the one desire of my heart He hadn't fulfilled, which was a husband to love me and do ministry with.

{Note: My husband and I were not saved when we got married. My salvation came the year after, yet, I honored my marriage and him: praying, fasting and believing for his salvation and service with me.}

I agreed with God to come back. But in light of my circumstances that followed, I felt this new husband prophecy was just a dream. But God. "The new thing." Right? "No longer forsaken," is what God would say to me every morning for the following months.

> "No longer will they call you deserted, or name your land desolate. But you will be called Hephzibah (The city of Gods delight), and your land Beulah ("The Bride of God"); for the Lord will take delight in you, and your land will be married." Isa 62:4

I began to bawl like a baby in front of my King. I whispered," God you know what they have said; you know how they all feel about me. But God, you see me."

> "She gave this name to the Lord who spoke to her: "You are the God who sees me", for she said, "I have now seen the One who sees me." Gen 16:13

This was the beginning of God and I's journey to wooing me back into a place of pure trust and faith. Believing for the impossible and believing that God desires to bless me and give me the desires of my heart. To be more than just my Master and my Savior, but now to be my Husband. A soulmate with a heart for God.

As I sat there on the beach, God began to talk about this natural man that was going to be my new husband. He asked me so softly and tenderly, "What do you want in a husband?"

I took a deep breath and said, "God I want a man that loves Wendy, the girl, knows my value and will be forever faithful to me. A man like you write about in Galatians 5:22-26:

> *"But the fruit of the spirit is love, joy, peace, forbearance, kindness, goodness, faithfulness, gentleness, and self-control. Against such things, there is no law. Those who belong to Christ Jesus have crucified the flesh with its passions and desires. Since we live by the Spirit, let us keep in step with the Spirit. Let us not become conceited, provoking and envying one another."*

And in Ephesians 5:25:

> *"Husbands, love your wives, just as Christ loved the church and gave himself up for her to make her holy, cleansing her by the washing with the water through the word."*

Most importantly, he will allow me to be me, to laugh with me, dance with me, cry with me and do life and ministry with me. I heard God laugh and say,

"Okay-okay, take a breath. Well, this man has the potential for all these, and his heart is good, but he is hard-headed. I need you to be patient as some of this will come in time, but all these characteristics exist in him. I want to give you a picture of him so that when you see him, you will know he is the one. Write this all down and keep it in your heart and mind:

- You will meet him in February.

- He is very tall

- He is Black, Tribe of Judah like you. He showed me a flag of green, yellow, and red with a lion on it (I looked up later. It was the flag of Ethiopia)

- He is younger than you

- He has matching tattoos on both arms (Huh? Tattoos really?) Then a picture popped in my head of an Egyptian eye

- He is very intelligent that sometimes gets in his way. You will help him with this.

- He has a past, but he has a calling on his life. He's not yet a minister

- He needs his inheritance now. Study the Old Testament to help him with his lineage

- He has a daughter brand new, not a wife.

- Hollywood, New York are important to him. Be ready to go to both

Here's the reason I chose you:

- He needs to know I love him enough to give him one of my most precious possessions, YOU.
- He needs affirmation. I will begin to fill you with so much love for him
- He will need the gift of tongues
- He will be sensitive to your health and eats a similar diet
- He is a truth seeker

I need him, Wendy. I need you to impart wisdom, hope, faith, and revelation into him.

You are capable of loving those with a past. He has one so just know I want to heal all of that.

He has a Joseph anointing and is the baby in his family. His heart is like David."

Wow, God, this is a lot. Thank you for choosing me, make me ready for all this. Protect my heart and bring him when he is ready."

God said, "Trust me, I got you. I am choosing Him because his heart is like yours. Before I put you both in your mothers' wombs, I let you meet each other. You will feel that soul connection when you meet him. He is your soulmate."

As God shared all this with me, I felt a tug on my heart. I felt a sense of honor that God chose me. My eyes filled with tears and my heart instantly felt whole again. I became so connected to God in the Spirit at that moment, all I could say is," Yes Lord, yes!, I trust you. Make me brave and ready to be his wife." I put the list in my bible and then took a much-needed walk on the beach.

Eric: Get Oouutt!

I was getting ready for another pointless night of work, when suddenly; a voice from my gut interrupted my misery and said, "It is time to leave that job."

"What??," I said out loud, "I can't do that. It's the most consistent thing in my life right now besides my laptop.

"It's time to go."

I knew it was a cry for help from within, but I squashed it down, finished dressing, and went on to work. This went on for months, and each time, it started to get louder and more incredulous.

"It is time to go."

"I will, just as soon as I get another commercial or sell a script. Then I'll be able to take care of myself and my daughter." More months passed and I didn't make a move.

One night that September, while I was kicking people out of the club at closing, a lady grabbed my hand and looked me in my eyes and said,

"You don't belong here."

I said, "Oh really? Okay." dismissing her because I thought she had a few drinks in her. As I pulled away to continue getting people out, she grabbed my hand tighter.

"No listen," she said emphatically, "You don't belong here. If you stay here, all of the people you are supposed to help will perish."

"Oh wow, ooo-kay."

She continued on saying she was a psychic and hadn't had a drink. "I promise you. I'm telling you, you don't belong here.

" I said, "I hear you, and I'm listening."

She gave me a stern look in my eyes to make sure I received what she said, then left with her friend. I continued getting people out, but I knew that was a "spiritual" moment. I may not have been an active church member, but my spirit knows God.

Quick Detour:

My family was religious. We couldn't listen to secular music on Sundays until noon. We said grace. My siblings and I had to honor our mother and father, etc.. I knew God and Jesus, but not The Holy Spirit. I knew OF the Father-Son-Holy Spirit trinity from

Catholic School, but not them as something real. When I was 8 years-old, I attended a Pentecostal Church in Virginia, and it was the first time I witnessed people catch the Holy Ghost. My friends and I laughed at the people who seemed to be having epileptic seizures and speaking gibberish. When I got home, somebody told my Dad that I was laughing at the people. He snatched me up in a New York minute and slammed me up against the wall. He glared into my eyes and said, "Don't you ever let me hear about you laughing at people in church again. Do you understand me?" "Yes," I said through sniffling and tears. And let's just say I haven't laughed in church since. That was my introduction to "getting drunk in The Spirit."

Months later, it would be my turn. I had a hunger for the Lord. I was watching people get baptized every week in the church, and my curiosity was stoked. I began wondering what are they doing? I kept hearing people say after they were baptized that they forgot all of their sins and were washed anew. I was 8, and I've done a few things that I wish I could forget, like lying about breaking my GI Joe doll. That was a big deal to me back then. I started wanting and praying to God, "I want to be baptized." Then one Sunday, I came home from church in tears. My mother said, "What's wrong?" I said, "I want to be baptized. Can I get baptized?" My mother said, "Sure, but why are you crying?" I said, "I didn't know if you would say yes." She just shook her head and gave me that motherly hug. I was baptized two weeks later, and my relationship with God began.

I finished closing up the club, still tingling from the psychic's words. As I walked down Sunset Blvd. at 3 am to the parking garage where my car was, my mind kept replaying her words, "You don't belong here. If you stay, all of the people you're supposed to help will perish...(echoing) perish-perish-perish."

Now I knew I had to get out of there. And to make sure the message was received loud and clear, God sent a confirmation. As I was walking, I glanced at an object in the middle of the street. Rectangular in shape. I was drawn to walk over to it. I picked it up. The book's title, "Scriptures For The Purpose Driven Life, by Rick Warren.

I stood there like a deer in front of a Mack truck's headlights. "What is going on?? Why is this happening to me?" The psychic's voice chimed in, "You don't belong here. If you stay, all of the people you're supposed to help will perish-perish-perish." The voice from my gut came back with a vengeance, "It's time to go."

I wanted to drop the book and run for the hills, but somehow, I knew "the universe" left it there for me. Frozen in shock, I thought to myself, "should I open it or not?" I chose not to open it, but I kept it and took it home. This is too much for one night.

It stayed on my desk for three days. Every time I passed it, I eyed with awe and trepidation. There's something in there for me, but I just wasn't ready to receive it. Finally, on the third day, I said, "Okay God, whatever you're trying to tell me, let me open to that page. I closed my eyes, took a deep breath, exhaled, and opened the book to a page. The scripture on the top of the page was from the book of Jeremiah 1:5.

> *"Before I formed you in the womb I knew you,*
> *before you were born I set you apart;*
> *I appointed you as a prophet to the nations."*

Holy prophet to the nations, Batman! Blood surged through my entire body. My heart started pounding. I started shaking. I sat down on my bed in shock. I just sat there, tears streaming down my eyes, thinking to myself, "What. Is. Going. On?"

CALL TO ACTION:

What event happened to you that you knew it was God telling you to do something? Did you do the thing He asked? If no, why not?

_____

_____

~CHAPTER THREE~

The Waiting Game

Wendy: The Dating Game

January came and went. February came and went. Nothing no word from God or this Man. I chose to let it go, feeling maybe it was my imagination. As I took the paper out of my Bible, I heard the Lord whisper, "He wasn't ready, but I need you to persevere." So, I prayed in tongues over the paper for about an hour and then put it away. God was making sure I knew I heard from HIM directly about this man. March came and went. April. May. June.

And then July. July was my birthday, so my girlfriends decided to set me up on a dating site. I said, "No," but they just laughed. They knew I never really dated. I got married at 18 years old, so I never had a lot of dating experience.

I saw myself as a pastor, not a woman who dates or is date-able. I was smart and had a great heart, but I never thought of myself as sexy or desirable like other women. Not because of low self-esteem, but more because I just saw myself as a 'warrior for God.' I had been consumed with God and not the world for so long, I just didn't think about that kind of stuff.

I ended up going out on a few dates to appease my girlfriends. I quickly decided this life was not for me. I was flooded with requests from men whose intentions had nothing at all to do with my assignment from God or my destiny. All dating did was help me gain unneeded opinions of myself and my relationship with God. So, I repented and shut the computer off.

My girlfriends were still scouting guys out, trying to play matchmaker. They were determined to help me out, sort of like an intervention. They did not understand what God had told me about Eric. And even when I would try to explain, they just did not get it.

I had attended a new church with some pastor friends of mine who had come into town. (Mind you this was my first time in church since I had lost my ordination). God said to me, "By the way, you are still my Apostle. "I began to weep. 'How God they see me as tainted," I cried. He gave me, Isa. 61:

> *"The Spirit of the Lord God is upon me; because the Lord hath anointed me to preach good tidings unto the meek; he hath sent me to bind up the brokenhearted, to proclaim liberty to the captives, and the opening of the prison to them that are bound; To proclaim the acceptable year of the Lord, and the day of vengeance of our God; to comfort all that mourn."*

The pastor preaching that night called me out of the seat and prophesied over me, "The best is yet to come. You are God's beloved whom he is well pleased with. Your latter days will be even greater. He is giving you a new name." I wept at the altar for what seemed to be an eternity. As I finally took my seat and opened my Bible to write it all down, the paper from God's talk at the beach about my husband fell out. I wrote the Pastors words on the back, and then God said, "I don't lie. Claim this husband." So, I did.

Then everything turned around. How many know that right before your blessing, in walks temptation, confusion and the counterfeit. But instead of recognizing it, I listened to the voice inside me saying, "I am lonely." I gave the enemy the open door he had been waiting for. So, I met someone. He seemed nice. I didn't stop and pray; I just thought 'oh wow, someone likes me.' After a while, I did ask God about the guy I was seeing, and he said, "NO". So, on November 1st, I just cried out, "God make me brave." I let the gentleman go and kept on moving forward with no other prospect insight.

{Note: Sometimes you just have to be okay with being alone with yourself; to believe and really walk out this thing called faith.}

"Now faith is the substance of things hoped for, the evidence of things not seen." Heb 1:11

Eric: You're Still Here??

"When anyone hears the message about the kingdom and does not understand it, the evil one comes and snatches away what was sown in their heart. This is the seed sown along the path." Mt 13:19

Two months later, I was still working at the club. I hadn't got another job, so I stayed. Knowing I had to get out of there, but couldn't, was frustrating. Not knowing anything about stepping out on faith, my disposition started to change. I was miserable. Things started to get under my skin that never bothered me before. I was in a flesh/spirit battle, and I had no idea what to do.

I called home to check in with my parents back in Maryland. As I was talking to my dad, he would ask what's going on with me. He could tell by my voice how I was doing, regardless of what I said.

Somewhere in the conversation, he would undoubtedly slip in, "Have you been going to church?" "Not that again," I would say under my breath. "No, I work Sundays," I'd answer him, hoping that would end this topic of conversation. He'd come back with, "Try to go once a month. You're a creative person. All of your answers are going to be there." How'd he know I was in need of answers? I'm doing just fine. "I got this," I would think defiantly. No Eric, you don't!

CALL TO ACTION:

What words did people prophesy over you that you ignored?

_____

_____

_____

_____

_____

~CHAPTER FOUR~

The Chance Encounter

Wendy: The Set up

A few days later, I was still trusting God for a lot. I had no job, and I was still working through my health issues. It was hard for me to believe God for all this and a husband. So, for the next week, I decided to fast and soak in worship. Then my girlfriend called and invited me down to visit her. (Little did I know what she was really up to at the time).

We drove down to Studio City. She said she needed to stop by

CVS before going to her house. She was talking about all the guys she had met online and how I needed to give it another try. I told her I wasn't really interested in playing games with these guys. She quickly changed the subject, parked the car by CVS, and we ran Inside to grab a few things. As we were coming out of the store, she said, "Hey, let's get a coffee since we're here." I said, "Okay."

As we were walking towards Starbucks, a white Maxima drives by super slow. I'm on automatic alert; I'm from Compton. Anyway, the car stops, the passenger window rolls down in slow motion. I hear a man's voice holler, "Wendy?"
What the??... I said, "YYYYes??" as I leaned down warily. The car then drove off to park. I whipped around and looked at my girlfriend. She had a huge devilish grin on her face and said,

"Don't be mad, but I set you up."

"Oh no, you diunt!"

She went on my site and planned this date with this guy! I'm stuck meeting this guy. Lord, give me skrenff! Yes, I said, "skrenff."

Just as I'm about to let her have it, he walks up to us. I said, "Hi," in my nice little church girl voice. He hugged my girlfriend and then me. I gave him the Christian side-hug. We proceeded to get a table, and he asks if he can buy us coffee. We gave him the order, and he goes inside. I laid into my girlfriend, "This poor dude thinks I wanted this. Now what?" She says I got this just be your sweet self. "Girl, I'm about to cut you," I murmured. She laughed. Two minutes later he comes out and says," Um I just forgot everything you guys told me. Will one of you come with me?" My girlfriend says, "Wendy will." So, I got up and went inside with him. We were instantly handsy as if we've been long lost friends,

{Side note: Yes, he is great looking. Yes, he seems very nice, but I know nothing about this guy! I was so caught off guard; I started praying in tongues in my head. But my body is acting like, "Hey, what's your name, sexiness". Lord help me. God gave me Isa 42:6:}

> "I the Lord have called thee in righteousness, and will hold thine hand, and will keep thee, and give thee for a covenant of the people, for a light of the Gentiles..."
> Is 42-6

I was like, "Really? God, what does that mean?" I hear God say, "Shhh have peace." We get back outside, and my girlfriend begins drilling him with questions. "Are you single?" "Yes," he said confidently. "Do you do drugs?" "No, never." "Are you looking for a girlfriend or a wife?" "Yes." "Okay, last question, do you love God and are you a Christian?" He says, "Oh most definitely. Saved since I was 8 years old". She's satisfied, so she excuses herself from the table, and now it's just Eric and I. As Tony the Tiger would say, Grrreat!

All of a sudden, I felt the Holy Spirit on me. I'm looking at Eric.

Our eyes lock, and something otherworldly just took over. I've never felt anything like this. I try making small talk, but he's not really responding. Then all of a sudden, he says, "You don't really look like your picture." I'm thinking, 'oh dear he's disappointed.' I guess my face told on me, because he says, "You're just way more beautiful in person." I said, "Thank you," and he reached his hand over to hold mine tightly. It was so amazing: the chemistry, the Holy Spirit, the peace of God that flooded me like a warm blanket around my shoulders. I heard God whisper, "I am right here." All of it felt like I was in a movie.

    I couldn't really talk. His eyes were telling me so much. Then all of a sudden, he says, "Can I please just kiss you so I can focus." Huh? Okay. I haven't dated much but is that really acceptable I just met him. (That's what my head said) My body just leaned over and kissed him. Oh my God!, I felt like a shock, a tingling on my lips. It was a wrap for me. I have no idea what he said after that. I was in love.

    Awhile later, my friend returned. She said, "Come on, we gotta go." I got up to leave. He held my hand, and my whole body got weak. When I got to the car, he just grabbed my face and planted a huge kiss on me, followed up by a huge hug. He lifted me off the ground! What is happening? We say goodbye. I get in the car, and

I am literally in shock. I can't even speak. My girlfriend looks over at me and says, "Just make sure I'm in the wedding." I laughed, but on the inside, I was all stirred up with emotions. God was all over me, and I was trying to make sense of it all. Later that night I prayed, and God said, "It's time." So, I began to pray in tongues, having no idea what "It's time" was referring to. It's amazing that after all God told me and prepared me for when it happened, I was not catching on. (I'm laughing at myself as I'm writing this.)

Eric: Divine Encounter Of The God Kind

I had been dating someone during this time, but she didn't know the deepest concerns I had. Now that I had no job and more time on my hands, I had to find ways to fill it. One way I bided my time was to join internet sites and have "a little fun" as I called it. I was on a couple of dating sites. I would click on women's profiles of all races and see where they lived. They couldn't live in LA or nearby. I wasn't serious; it was just fun. I had no intention of meeting any of them in person. I'll have a web cam camera convo with them, talk the talk, then when if it got to the point of wanting to meet, I'd go AWOL.

Quick Detour:

I'm a good conversationalist, so meeting people and keeping them engaged is not a problem for me. Some would say I'm charismatic, others would say I'm a Play-a. I'm somewhere in the middle. I can be whatever I need to be at the time. For instance, I was more interested in finding a way to get their phone number without the intent of calling. It was the hunt, solving the puzzle, unlocking the key to each woman's heart. My main weapon was... humor. As I'm writing this, my dad's wisdom convicts me, "Just because you can, doesn't mean you do it." Meaning just because I can get girls with my charm, doesn't mean I use my personality gifts for evil, manipulation, etc..

> "I did not give you the spirit of fear, but of power, of love, and of self-control." 2 Tim 1:7

This went on for some time until I discovered this new site. I was like "Ah, fresh meat." I started down the same path as before, adding 1500 women from all walks of life to my e-black book. One day, I clicked on this woman's profile that lived about an hour's drive north from my apartment.

She was beautiful, had an amazing smile, and by my man vision, I could tell from her picture she had some curves. Men know what I'm talking about. I sent her a heart letting her know I was interested. She responded days later with a heart. Nice. I remember what struck me most about her profile was she stated on her page, "God has my heart. You have to get the key to it from Him." A church girl. Hmm, do I want to mess with this? My ego says, "Go ahead; you can talk that religious talk." We played internet tag for a while, months even. Then one day she sent me a note stating she'll be down in my area to visit a friend. I wrote back, "Let's meet up." Something came up for her, and she canceled. More months passed, then I get a message from her that she's coming down to see her same friend this weekend. I wrote back, "Let me know when you get here..." I started to get anxious. I had to meet her. Wait, I'm breaking my own rule, "Just talk to them; don't meet in person!" But something about her just made me have to meet her.

We decided to meet at Starbucks in Studio City by her friend's house on Saturday. I couldn't sleep Friday night. I was anxious. I don't get anxious about many things, but I was officially anxious. I woke up Saturday, cleaned my white Maxima SE. At 3:45, I hopped in my car and made the fifteen-minute drive over to the Starbucks. As I was driving, I berated myself,

"You're not supposed to meet them in person. Don't flirt too much. And don't leave with her".

"I'm not-I'm not."

I pulled into the parking lot and did the slow drive-by of Starbucks to see if I saw her. I was hoping she resembled her picture by say 85%, you know how pictures go. They'll show you a picture from six years ago and be mad at you when you have a problem with it. I saw this woman standing near the outside patio of Starbucks: curves stuffed in tight jeans, open toe heels, a black Baby Phat shirt, curly hair, just waiting there. DAAAYYYYUUMMM, is that her?? I slowed to a crawl as I powered down the passenger side window.

"Wendy?"

"Hi," she said angelically.

Wow, she's way hotter than her picture. My ego went crazy.'Uh-oh, E, you messed up now."

I tried to play cool, but I couldn't park my car fast enough. I parked, checked my hair, (I can hear Wendy laughing her butt off when she reads this... inside joke), lips for ash, fresh breath. We good; let's go. No pressure. Enjoy yourself dawg.

I approached her, and we hugged. Oh my god, she was so soft. She smelled so good. Her eyes sparkled. Her hair, a radiant reddish blond. Uh-oh, I think I done messed up and fell in love.

Her friend was sitting at the table. Wendy and I sat down next to each other. We were handsy instantly; holding hands, resting our hands on each other's arms and legs, high-fiving. It was crazy.

And another non-manly word is about to come out of my mouth. My body started tingling with attraction. Butterflies fluttered in my stomach. This girl done turned me into a Harlequin romance novel. I thought people said those phrases just to make their 'how they met story' interesting. It never happened to me to this level. I've been attracted to people, but not to this extent. What is going on??

After exchanging pleasantries, the friend changed gears. She became, "The Investigator." As Wendy and I sat there like kids being interrogated by their parents before a first date, The Investigator started hurling questions at me in rapid succession. I'm answering them succinctly and to the point. I was passing with flying colors until the friend leaned forward dramatically and asked, "Do you believe in God?" And like clockwork, I said, "Of course. I'm all about God. I was saved at eight. He's been with me all the time." A lot of truth with a little lie. I wasn't all about God. I was just a believer. I still hadn't been to church at this time.

I kept looking at her and looking at her and looking at her. Pinch me. The curves. The smile. There was so much attraction going on; I couldn't think. I literally asked her, "Excuse me, may I kiss you? I can't think or hear anything you're saying right now because I need to kiss you." I know it sounds like a line, but it wasn't. I was dead serious.

She said, "Yes."

I leaned in; her soft lips met mine with the perfect amount of pressure. And for-real for-real, I heard an angelic choir singing, "Ahhh Ahh Ahhh Ahhh Ahhh."

I can't remember anything after that. I remember holding her hand to order a drink; I remember walking her to her car, framing her face with my hands and giving her a passionate kiss. As I watched her and her friend drive away, I knew something very real just happened.

CALL TO ACTION:

When was the moment you knew your spouse was 'the one?'

_____

_____

_____

~CHAPTER FIVE~

Three-Day Honeymoon

Wendy: It Is Him

So, the next day I got up and went to try a new church with my girlfriend and have lunch. I shared with her all through lunch about the word God gave me back in January about a husband. My subconscious was talking to her, but my head was still not connecting the dots for me. She knew I was smitten so later, unbeknownst to me, she contacted Eric and asked him if he could take me home for her. When she was leaving for work the next morning, she says, 'Oh, by the way, I have to work late, so I asked Eric to take you home." What? Who? "Are you kidding me? What is wrong with you?," I said to her. She just laughed, hugged me and skipped out the door.

I began packing and getting ready when I get a call on the home phone; It's him! Be cool. Be cool. I'm a lady. "Hi, I am here," he said. Oh my gosh, I was so nervous. I grabbed my bags and headed down the stairs. What am I doing? This is crazy. I was beyond nervous. Why you may ask? In case I didn't mention it before or you forgot, the chemistry I felt with this man was off the charts. I never in my life felt something physical like this for someone, anyone. (Help me ladies, I am trying to keep my salvation here) Plus, did I mention he's beautiful and sweet?

So, he greets me at the door and says hello and gives me another great big hug and kiss. I just felt so safe and at ease in his arms. He looked me deep in my eyes, and I felt this connection with him like I have known him my whole life. He puts me in the car like a true gentleman, loads my bags, and we're off. The reggae music is playing. We're laughing and telling jokes to each other. And then he asks me how soon do you have to be home? I said, "I have no time restrictions." He says, "Can we stop by my house for a quick second?" I said, "Sure," like it was nothing. (I am starting to see why chaperons were invented. I am straight gahgah right now!) So, we get to his house, and he says, "Come in with me. I don't want you outside waiting." So, I just get out and follow him inside. My whole life I've waited for a man who knew how to lead and my body just responded to his calm and take-charge ways. Now I know why. We were having a divine appointment that neither of us was really in charge of.

I sat down. He offered me some tea, turned the TV on, (which neither of us was watching) and then as if we had been together forever, he reaches down, grabs my feet, puts them in his lap, slides my shoes off, and begins rubbing my feet! {Ladies, come on right!} All the while, he's talking to me about college, sports, religion and numerous other topics. The conversation was seamless we could talk on literally any subject and relate to each other. And then it hits me, this man is rubbing my feet! 'Oh dear God, I got to get out of here!' is what my head was saying, but my body for some reason was no longer in agreement with my mind.

We talked so long I didn't realize it was dark outside. We have not eaten all day. He says, "It looks late, are you hungry? Um hello, I have literally been here all day into the evening and you're asking me if I am hungry? But all I said to him was, "Sure, I guess." So, we discussed dietary needs I had and then that led us to talk about the

Daniel fast, and then it hits me, "Oh God. God, is this?" God says loud and strong, "YES, this is him. Your husband." Wait What!!!

Eric was now sitting on the floor showing me some of his book collection, and so I ask him, "Are you familiar with the flag of..." He finishes my sentence, "Ethiopia?" I said, "Um yes." He opens a box and pulls out a large red, green and gold beach towel of the flag. My whole body began to tremble. Then I looked at his arms and realized he has matching tattoos of Egyptians eyes. Now the list is playing in my head. Eric is still talking to me, and we're communicating, but my brain was in full recall mode of the list God gave me. "Oh God, am I ready for this? Wow, God, seriously am I ready?" God says, "Yes."

Eric goes on to tell me about him and his family living in Turkey. He's the youngest. It's like he's literally reading my own list back to me. I got a tunnel-like vision and a deja vu type thing happening all at once like my mind, body, and soul. So, I asked him straight out, "Do you feel like you have a call on your life? He stopped what he was doing, looked me straight in the eye for what seemed to be a lifetime, then says, "Why do you ask?" I shrugged my shoulders trying to get my barrings. It's not like I am going to just blurt it out because I think you are my husband or anything.

So, he sits down next to me and says I need to share something crazy with you. He began telling me how he worked at a nightclub and a lady told him he didn't belong there, and then he found a book, The Purpose Driven Life, in the middle of the street (This is for real happening to me right now). He then proceeds to tell me how he has always loved God and seeks the truth, but that he was not religious or a churchgoer.

[Hindsight: Right here, I should have prayed with him, and asked him to take me home. However instead...]

I grabbed his face this time and kissed him long and hard. There was so much passion and excitement happening all at the same time. I just com-busted right then, and we ended up tearing each other's clothes off and going into the bedroom to make love.

Lesson: Now listen, I am human. Yes, I gave into my flesh and no, I am not condoning this behavior. However, I am sharing this story not only to be transparent but to show you that even a seasoned Christian can have moments of weakness.

Eric: Southern Hospitality

A couple of days later, I received a call from her friend, saying that she couldn't take Wendy home and could I. "Helll Yeah!" I exclaimed in my head. But on the phone, I was Arctic cool, "Sure, I can move some stuff around." She gave me the time and the address to pick her up in the morning.

I was there ten minutes early. Making sure I wouldn't start out with a negative mark against me. I called her, and she said she was ready. As I was heading up to the friend's apartment, she came walking down the stairs in a jean outfit. Two words: Yum. Mee. I took her overnight bags, set them in my car, opened my car door for her, and we drove off.

I lived 10 minutes from the friend's house, so I told her I had to stop by my apartment for a minute. I promised her this was not a trick. She was fine with it. We went to my house. Once inside, we sat on the couch. I made her some hot green tea and asked her what time she needed to be home?

She said, "I'm not in a hurry."

"Oh, okay, well we can sit here and watch a little Tv," I said, delighted.

"Okay," she said.

I turned it on, and we sat next to each other on the couch talking about something. We started talking and laughing like old friends. She was cracking me up. She's really funny. Very important to a comedian to have a woman who can make him laugh. I played my reggae music, espoused about my favorite Rastafarian artists, and showed her my "Lion Of Judah" beach towel. Things I don't just show anybody. She loved all of it. We also realized we both eat very healthy. She had common sense and knew a lot of things about various subjects. Is she real? This is too crazy. Everything was going so smooth.

As the day turned into night, all types of lust-filled emotions were coursing through my veins. I didn't want to move too fast. Remember I told her before she came into my apartment that we would just be chilling for a moment. I didn't want her to think I was giving her a line because I wasn't. But the more we sat, talked and laughed, the more that voice in my head kept chirping, "do this, kiss that, do the fake yawn and reach your arm around her neck move." I gave her my word, but I was weakening in her presence. Once all of the emotions came to ahead, I had to do something. I berated myself, "Either get her in the car and take her home or go against my word." Let me tell y'all, I wasn't taking her home until she said she was ready to go home. At that very moment, her legs were across mine on the couch, and I gazed at her perfectly-pedicured toes and said, "Eureka! I've got it. I'll give her a foot massage." I asked her, "May I do something? Trust me; you'll like it." She said, "Okay."

So, I went and got some cocoa butter lotion, removed her shoes and started giving her a foot massage. Many of you may think this was a playa move, and normally it would be. But as I began massaging her feet, a warm tingling sensation came over me. Not again! My whole body started quivering. The more I massaged her, the stronger the tingling became. Tears literally came to my eyes as I moved on to the other foot. What is going on? Why am I feeling all of this? There's no way this is happening. But the more I continued, it was like we were melding into one. It sounds crazy, but it's the truth. This was no normal foot massage. This one had meaning, purpose, and destiny behind it. As I finished, I looked into her eyes again, and she had this smile that radiated like a heavenly angel. And I had to kiss her at the moment, and so I did. That led to us kissing and moving the festivities to my bedroom. ..

CALL TO ACTION:

Name the 5 most amazing moments after you met your spouse while you were dating?

_____

_____

_____

_____

_____

_____

~CHAPTER SIX~

The Calling

Wendy: Yes Lord

I woke up early-early in the morning and was sitting there watching him sleep. I said wholeheartedly, "God, please forgive me for my weakness; I am truly sorry. But God, look at him; I just had no idea he would be… ." I heard God say, "All is forgiven; let it go." Tears streamed down my face. This man was so tender and kind and so perfect for me. I started to pray in tongues as to not wake him. God said, "Put your finger on his wrist." So, I did and then just closed my eyes and prayed. A few minutes later, I hear Eric whisper out loud, "Yes God, I hear you." Oh my goodness, what is happening? Eric says, "Yes, God', two more times and then opens his eyes and says to me, "What are you doing?" "Huh," I said, "I am not doing anything, why"? He sat up and said, "I just heard God audibly! Tears rolled down our faces, and we hugged ever so tightly.

After that experience, all my walls came tumbling down. He made me breakfast; then he took me to see the Michael Jackson documentary movie. We held hands, strolled down Hollywood Blvd. He showed me all his favorite music at his favorite music store. We listened to music for hours just laughing, touching and having fun. Then we went to eat and as we were walking a man (homeless) was standing by the light where we were going to cross. I said in my head, "I don't have any cash on me." Right as I said it in my head, Eric pulls out some cash and hands it to him. I said to him, "I was hoping you would do that."

At the restaurant, we were talking about travel and our future together as if we had been dating for years. And I just blurted out, "Oh and I am ready to move to New York." Eric looked at me for a long second, not saying a word. As soon as we got up to leave Eric pulled me by the waist and kissed me and said, "Thank you," in my ear. Wow, this is how easy it is when it's God I thought to myself.

I stayed with Eric for the next two days. Yes, I did. Each day we listened to music, talked about life and culture and God. We were sharing our hearts and our deepest secrets with each other. We cleaned out his closet and took a bunch of new clothes to the shelter, then we went to the beach and read the Word where God had Eric re-baptized himself in the ocean water. I watched with tears in my eyes as Eric was standing in the water with his hands extended to heaven as he fully surrendered to God. We stayed till dark holding each other, kissing each other and reading the Word together. This had to be God. We went to the grocery store, and I made him dinner. It was literally effortless.

By the third day, my girlfriend had called Eric and was like, "Um, what happened to Wendy? She never made it home?" He just grinned and handed me the phone. I began sharing with her what had happened. My girlfriend hears from God as well, so it was no surprise to her. In fact, her comment remained consistent, "Just make sure I'm in the wedding." I laughed, and we said goodbye. It was kind of a jolt. Eric and I had been in our own little cocoon. So, I called my mom and told her what was going on. She too became excited and could not wait to meet him. After that, we prayed, and we decided I should go home, so begrudgingly, Eric took me home.

He took me to my mom's house where he met my mom and my stepdad. We all laughed and talked for a while, and then he said, "I guess I should get back." My heart stopped, but I said, "Okay."

I got in my car and headed to my own home. When I got there, I could not wait to give him a call. Once I did, we talked and laughed for about an hour, then said goodbye. Not even 20 minutes later I got a call back," I miss you, and I want to come back for you." I grinned from ear-to-ear and said, "Okay," and he did. When we got back to his place, Eric says, "I just got a whole download from God before I came to pick you up." As I walked over to him, he had the most amazing glow to him, like a little boy who just met his all-time favorite hero. He handed me the paper, and I read it. It had all kinds of notes pertaining to movies and life, but then I look down at the one with a giant star next to it, and it says, "Wendy is your wife." Oh my God, what do I say now? I'm thinking in my head. God fill my mouth. I looked at Eric, and I said, "How do you feel about all this? Eric says, "I feel grrreat! I feel like I found my purpose!"

Ooo-kay, I thought to myself. Then he got up out of the chair and hugged me super tight and gave me a long passionate kiss. I was pure jello by now. We prayed over the things on his paper, and for a job for me. Praying with Eric seemed so natural and so effortless, I really felt like I could be me.

Eric: Wake Up It's Me, God

The next morning, we were fast asleep. I'd later find out that I was the only one asleep, but I digress. Around 6 am, I was awakened by a powerful, authoritative voice. At first, I thought I was dreaming.

He said, "Eric, wake up. Wake up, Eric."

I didn't right away, but the Voice kept talking.

"Eric, you belong to me now. You are mine, do you understand me?" The Voice was so authoritative, I literally spoke out loud, "Yes."

As The Voice kept talking, I said to Wendy because she was up now, "What are you doing?" She didn't answer me as The Voice kept talking out loud in my room! My eyes are open, and I'm awake and The Voice is talking!

"You are to write the stories I tell you to write, do you understand me?

"Yes."

"I will do mighty things through you, do you understand?

"Yes."

This went on for another two or three minutes, and then The Voice vanished. I sat up in my bed trying to wrap my brain around what just happened. I looked at Wendy, and she had this sheepish grin on her face. "What just happened?," I said

"What? I didn't do anything?"

"Right, what did you do?"

Later, I found out she was praying over me for hours as I slept and God told her to touch my wrist. When she did, God started speaking to me. The God Of The Universe, Jehovah, Yahweh, The Great I Am spoke to me!!! After coming back to reality, the first thing I did was call my mom back in Maryland. I said, "Mom, guess what? I just heard the voice of God." Thinking she would be overly ecstatic, she replied with her steady demeanor, "Is that so?" I told her the things God said to me, and she said,

"Did you write them down?"

"No, I was out of my mind at the time. The Creator of The Universe spoke to me!!"

I was on cloud twelve the next few days. One, because of that God thing that happened, and two, Wendy ended up staying with me for the next three days. Yes, three days. We had a blast.

One morning during the three-day honeymoon, I received my

first download from God. A download is when God starts talking to you about his plans for your life, the week, the day, the hour. I was ready this time. I grabbed a pad and pen and scribbled as fast as humanly possible. He told me about my movie scripts selling, my next job, things I have to work on, but the main thing he told me was, "Wendy is your wife," I remember putting a star by that one. We went to Santa Monica beach where God had me baptize myself in the ocean. We read scriptures while sitting in the sand as the sunset. Then we went out to eat and rented movies from Blockbuster (I miss Blockbuster). We even went to see Michael Jackson's last movie; *This Is It*!

Revelation:

Up until us writing this book, Michael Jackson's movie was just that, a movie. But now we realize that God was trying to tell us something. "This Is It!"

After seeing it, we were hungry, so we went across the street to a Baja Fresh. As we were waiting for the light to turn green, there was a down-on-their-luck person (I hate the word bum) nearby. I reached into my pocket and gave him some money. Wendy squeezed my arm and said, "I was hoping you would do that."

While we were eating at Baja, we laughed and joked about things, talked about the movie, and then she said something so simple that it just made me know she's the one. She said, "... And when you're ready to move back to NY, I'm ready to go." Here's the magic in those words. I never told her I was thinking about moving back to New York though I was, AND, that was one of the things God told me during my download. I never told her either thing, yet she was on-board. But God!

Finally, on the third day, Wendy received a phone call. "Where are you?!" the voice shrieked from within the phone. It was her family calling worried sick about her, wondering where she was. We were so engulfed in our own little Garden of Eden paradise, we forgot about the rest of the world. And we didn't care. We came to the conclusion that we better finally make that trip home so everyone could see she was fine and to prove she was not kidnapped or on the side of the road dead somewhere.

After meeting her family, I was ready to go (not really), so we said our goodbyes, kissed and I started to head back to my house. I got a call in the car. She wanted to go with me. I turned around, scooped her up, and we went back to my house.

CALL TO ACTION:

What was a word that God gave you that you are running from?

_____

The Prodigal Couple

_____
_____
_____
_____

~CHAPTER SEVEN~

Coming Up For Heir

Wendy: Everything Was Falling Into Place

    The days just flew by, and our connection just kept getting stronger. Every time we would pray and go do something, some kind of event would take place. We both were hearing from the Lord separately and would say what the other heard; it was crazy. By the end of the weekend, God was like, "Okay, time to go." I knew God was a part of all this, except the part where we were not able to keep our hands off each other. We were not lusting after each other, we were both like, well like feeling like our lives were becoming whole. We felt what each other was feeling, and I could tell he was being fully transparent with me about things he never spoke to anyone else about. He was the best friend God promised me and so much more, but it was time. So, he packed me up and took me home for the second time.

The next morning, I got a call for a job, and by Tuesday I had a job. My life was finally lining up. I had Eric and now a new job. I could not wait to tell him. Dear God, I am madly head over heels in "LOVE." Not just with this man, but with my God who hand-picked him just for me.

Eric: Drop That Bible-Base

We started seeing each other regularly. Wendy got her new job at a local college and I started working on a powerful trilogy that the Lord had downloaded to me while I was unemployed. My daughter was living in Chicago with her mom at the time, and it was very painful time to be away from her. I missed all of her firsts: walking, talking, and climbing out of the crib. All of those moments that make becoming a parent worthwhile. I can't worry about that now; I have to keep it moving. God got me.

Wendy sent me scriptures and prophetic words from God almost daily. I remember a few in particular because they had a recurring theme. She would say, "God says you're going to have a five-fold ministry." "A five-fold what?" she had so much faith in the man I was supposed to be.

> *"So, Christ himself gave the apostles, the prophets, the evangelists, the pastors, and teachers, to equip his people for works of service, so that the body of Christ may be built up." Eph 4: 11-13*

God was telling me I would be an apostle, evangelist, pastor, teacher, and prophet. Prophet? Where did I see that word before? Jer 1:5:

> *"Before I formed you in the womb I knew [you before you were born I set you apart; I appointed you as a prophet to the nations..."*

DING-DING-DING, confirmation. I can't lie; it's hard to see myself going from a stand-up comedian/writer/actor to an apostle, pastor, prophet, evangelist, and teacher for God, even to this day. I didn't go to seminary school or live the 'church life.' My life was built around being an entertainer, not a pastor. But if God is coming after me like this, I have to take notice. He had my undivided attention.

I started to search for churches to go to. After a couple of visits to local churches, I landed at a church in Culver City where many entertainers attended. The pastor was one of the featured pastors in the movie, "The Secret." I went to the services a couple of times, and it wasn't bad. He gave good sermons that sparked things within me. I told Wendy I was going to his church, thinking she'd be impressed. She asked me one question that rained on my parade. She asked me was it a Bible-based church? Not really. It's more metaphysical, self-realization type stuff with a little Jesus mixed in. "You need a Bible-based church." (sigh) "Fine, I don't really know the difference, but okay."

"In the beginning was the Word, and the Word was with God, and the Word was God. He was with God in the beginning. Through him all things were made; without him, nothing was made that has been made. In him was life, and that life was the light of all mankind. The light shines in the darkness, and the darkness has not overcome it." John 1: 1-4

CALL TO ACTION:

What things did you do daily when you were on fire for the Lord?

_____

_____

_____

~CHAPTER EIGHT~

Acceleration!

Eric: Let The Healing Begin

Wendy started leading a bible study over at her friend's house on Tuesdays and 'asked' me to join in. I did of course, so that next Tuesday, I arrived at the friend's apartment where a quaint group of her friends were gathering. As soon as I entered, Christian Rock worship music punched me in the face and Wendy was on her knees passionately worshiping the Lord. I was like, "Uh-oh, she ain't playing in here." When she finished worshiping and praying in tongues, (I didn't laugh, I promise), Wendy started teaching. The Word and the words flowed out of her mouth like water. She knew what she was talking about and it was obvious she knew God, intimately. I was mesmerized by her passion and fiery tone. The Word is serious business to her. She loves God and has suffered many trials during her walk with God.

They called her Pastor Wendy and treated her with so much reverence and respect. I was truly turned on watching her in her environment. Ain't nothing sexier than a woman living out her purpose with passion, right fellas? I was enjoying learning the Word from her, that is until she started trying to throw some responsibility onto me. I was like "No thank you. Do you." I didn't say that exactly, but that's what I felt. She couldn't care less. When prophetic words came to me, she made me speak them. She made me lay hands on people. She made me pray for people. That was the hardest. How do you pray for people you don't know, and you don't have the prayer verbiage down just yet. "Um, I speak peace and uh... love and um... soul over you. Amen? Lol.

One week later, she got a call that her stepfather was in the hospital sick with heart and lung issues. I drove her up to see him at the hospital. The doctors told her she could go into his room. She rose, and I stayed seated. She reached back and said, "Come on, we have to pray for him." "We?" (sigh) I stood and followed her into the room.

Her dad was hooked up to various breathing machines. I can't lie, I hate hospitals and seeing him like that freaked me out. He was happy to see her as he struggled to open his eyes. After giving him encouraging words, Wendy said, "Do you want us to pray over you?" He nodded his head weakly. Wendy grabbed my hand and laid them on her dad's chest. Within seconds, her dad started coughing.

She anointed his head and feet with oil and began to pray over him. Suddenly, his heart rate began to stabilize, and his wheezing started clearing up. What the hell?! I'm watching this happen right before my eyes! When we came in, he could barely muster up a whisper. By the time we left, he was speaking normally. The next day, Wendy gave me his praise report that he was fine and going home. The water in his lungs left overnight, and his swollen limbs were almost back to normal size. What?? This prayer stuff really works! Wendy is a powerful woman in God. She tried to say it was us, but it was God and her. I was just a participant. A very lucky and grateful witness to a move of God.

If I didn't believe what happened to her stepfather, then the Lord, in his great wisdom, set up another divine appointment to ingrain it in me. We went out to eat at a restaurant and ran into a guy who had some serious back pain. He was hurting and had no insurance to get help. Wendy grabbed her oil from her purse, rubbed it on our hands, and we prayed over that guy. Minutes later, he could bend and touch his toes and twist. God Is. Just crazy. I was just like Gideon now. "I saw you do that, Lord, but just so I know it's really you, can you do it again? Pleeaassee."

He obliged. Weeks later, Wendy and I prayed for her co-worker at her job who had been diagnosed with cancer. What do you think happened? Yep, the doctors found no sign of cancer on her next check-up. God is 3-for-3. "God, I'm in. I've seen all I've needed to see."

Wendy: Serving God

Everything was seemingly falling right into place. We found each other, we both clearly heard God. We had amazing encounters with God. We were leading people to Christ, healing the sick, and building a ministry team in record time. We already had a Bible study meeting weekly with people Skyping in from Alaska to San Diego. Then all of a sudden, the shift occurred. No longer was he sitting on the phone with me for hours at a time or calling me back right away. It was all too familiar to me from my past. However, I was standing on my promises from God and trying not to let my past control my thoughts for the future. I knew that I knew that he was my husband and that this is God's intent for our lives, so I began to press in. Doing what I like to call a temperature read with God. I wanted to make sure all my ducks were in a row and that this was not just me. So, I called my intercessors and had them begin to pray. I fasted. I finally spoke to him and he reassured me that everything was good and that he was just busy writing.

CALL TO ACTION:

What offense made you get off the path God had you on?

_____

_____

_____

_____

~CHAPTER NINE~

Redding Is Calling

Wendy: Denied Tres Times

I phoned Eric and asked him if he wanted to go up north with me. His response was, "Yes, but I will drive myself." Boom!, the bomb dropped. I chose not to give into fear and just pressed into God. On my drive up north, I listened to worship and really pressed in to hear the voice of the Lord. "God, is this not who you said would be my husband?" God said, "Yes." "Okay then, what is going on?" God said, "Eric is entrapped to his past. Keep still and watch and see this weekend."

My great friends and spiritual Mother and Father attend this church. I stayed with them and began to share my heart and about Eric. I was searching for answers. I went to bed early after an 8-hour drive and decided to wait on God as he instructed. However, every part of who I am was screaming inside, "Please God protect my heart and the work you have begun through us."

The next day I got up early and went to the chapel. I prayed in tongues for what seemed to be an eternity. This church is very blessed in the prophetic and I wanted to make sure my heart and mind were right and ready to receive all that God had for me. God just kept reassuring me of his love for me and how precious I was to him. He kept calling me his beloved. After service, I felt at peace. The worship was amazing. Eric had finally arrived and seemed normal enough to me, so I just thought I have been overreacting. So, I repented and moved forward to the area where you could get individual prayer. I was with Eric, my close girlfriend and my spiritual parents.

When it was our turn for prayer, the first woman to speak said, "You and your husband have greatness inside you." The lady continued to speak over me that God was rewarding me for my faithfulness. "He is restoring your uterus and ovaries so that you can give your husband a child." As the lady continued to pray in tongues, Eric said softly under his breath, "This is just my friend. Wait, What?!! My friends looked at me and said, "We'll see you back at the house," and left. The ladies continued to pray over Eric and give him words as well. God gave me Acts 13:22:

> "After removing Saul, he made David their king. He testified concerning him: "I have found David son of Jesse a man after my own heart; he will do everything I want him to do."

God said to me, "Things are not as they seem. Trust me. I trust Him. He is a man after my own heart like David. Speak that over him, not what you see." Right then, as I was obedient, Eric let out this gut-wrenching cry. God said," Today, you helped birth his spirit man. Thank you, Wendy, for being obedient."

Eric: Shaken & Stirred

Wendy rounded up the bible study group and told us we needed to make a trip up to Bill Johnson's powerful Bethel Church in Redding, CA, about 8 hours North of LA, during the July 4th holiday weekend. This church was known as a healing church with the thick presence of God living there. I never heard of the church, Bill Johnson, or the city of Redding. But Wendy thinks we should go, so we're going. I drove up by myself on July 3. Wendy was coming up with a couple of the group members before me. She was staying at her Pastor friends' home. On July 4th, I got to the church and met up with Wendy and the group just as the 11 am service began. It was a great service. The sermon was about the "incorruptible seed" by assistant pastor, Danny Silk. It was powerful. He talked about the devil comes to steal your identity, purpose, and destiny. It hit me right between the eyes. I still look over the notes from that sermon to this day.

Afterwards, we were on our way out when a tall Jewish lady came right up to me and said, "The Lord told me I'm supposed to pray for you." I said, "Okay." She told me to stretch out my hands. I did. She put her hands under mine. She firmly squeezed them and started praying. She shook my hands as if trying to break something off of me and intensified her praying. Suddenly, my body began to quiver from my toes up. She kept praying. My shaking intensified. I started crying. Prayer warriors at the church joined in. They laid hands on me and starting shouting out bible chapters. One said, "Isaiah 42." Another said, "Psalms 91." Another, "Romans 8." I'm shaking, crying, snot crying, yes, snot crying. She started prophesying, "You are going to the nations!" Oh no, the Lord says you're going to the world. I am taking you to the world!"

> *"Before I formed you in the womb I knew you*
> *before you were born I set you apart;*
> *I appointed you as a prophet to the nations..."*

This went on for at least another 45 minutes! When I finally came to, I was sloshed in the spirit, forget drunk. I needed to go to HSA – Holy Spirit Anonymous. "Hi, my name is Eric, and I'm a Holy Spirit-aholic. Whoo-hoo!" The lady's last words to me were, "We just broke a lot of stuff off of you. You are free now." I felt free. Free from what, I don't know, but if this is what freedom feels like, sign me up! I wish I could remember half of the things she prophesied over me that day. All I can really remember is the trembling, shaking, and snot crying. The Holy Spirit slammed me hard that day. Real hard. Happy Independence Day to me. I just hope nobody was laughing at me.

Wendy: Jilted

When we were done, we went back to my pastor's home. He was like a protective father. He shook Eric's hand. He and his wife, my spiritual mother, looked at me and said, "Come, let's go into the den and talk." My spiritual Mom put out her hand, and I gave her mine. She began praying in tongues. Tears rolled down my face as the Pastor gently looked me in the eyes and said, "Who is this man to you?" I said, "I believe he is my husband that God brought me." He then looked at Eric with some concerns in his face and asked him a series of questions about his relationship to God, and ministry, and life. Then the bomb hit. He looked right at Eric and said, "Who is this woman to you?" Eric said, matter-of-factly, "She is my friend. My very good friend."

I began to tremble. He literally sucker-punched me in the gut, and it took all of my being to not fall on the floor. The pastor's wife began to hold me, and the Pastor escorted Eric out of the room. They began to soak me in prayer.

Quick Detour:

My spiritual parents had been with me for a lot of my journey; they knew the hell I had endured in my previous marriage. They knew I believed God for a mighty man of God. They were interceding for a man worthy of me for over 10 years, so this hurt them both as much as it was hurting me. However, they were not about to let the Devil have me, or my heart.

_____

Eric left, and I stayed for another day. I could barely get out of the bed. The pastor of the church and his wife came over as well to pray and lay hands on me. My mind was racing as well as my heart, "But God you said he is the one. What happened? What did I do?" All four of them one by one told me my worth and that I deserved better than this. You must know that you are "Priceless" to God. I knew God loved me; I knew God used me; I knew I loved God. Priceless, not so much. I was always settling for almost.

As I packed my bags to head home, my spiritual mom said these words which I will never forget. "Wendy Darline, you are God's rarest jewel. You have allowed God to change you, teach you and grow you. You are an overcomer and so much more. Your Father in heaven wants to brag on you, show you off. And only a man after God's own heart will be rewarded with the gift of you. Do not give yourself away." Wait, what?? "A man after God's own heart," That's exactly who God told me Eric was!

I decided to forgive Eric and put my trust in God. The whole trip home, I soaked in God through worship and waited for instructions on what to do next. Meanwhile, my intercessor and friend, Bethany, called me and said that God gave her a word for Eric about counterfeit and confusion. I told her she should call him directly. When she was done, she called back and said: "Are you aware he is now referring to you as just a friend?" I said, "Yes, just pray." I fell to my knees and surrendered him and all of this to God. "Oh God, if I started this ministry too soon please forgive me and watch over all these people, so they do not get hurt." God replied, "Thank you, now trust me. Watch and see what I will do next."

CALL TO ACTION:

When were you at your lowest point?
_____
_____
_____
_____

How did you call on God?
_____
_____
_____
_____

~CHAPTER TEN~

On Fire For God!!

Eric: Stripped To The Bone

I came back from Redding fired up for The Lord. I was reading the bible more, praying more, using my new prayer language like a boss. But nobody tells you the flip side of this lifestyle is now you have to live holy. That means all things in your life that are abominations to God have to go. When Wendy explained this to me, I was fine with it because I had my own version of what it meant. I don't steal, kill, drink, smoke, do drugs, cheat, watch porn

– Ehhhh!, wrong answer. I did watch porn occasionally. I had a few gigs on my hard drive. I also had what I learned to be occult books that I used for writing. Had to go. Anything that was idolic in nature had to go.

"You shall have no other gods before Me. You shall not make for yourself any idol or any likeness (form, manifestation) of what is in heaven above or on the earth beneath or in the water under the earth [as an object to worship]. You shall not worship them nor serve them; for I, the Lord your God, am a jealous (impassioned) God [[a]demanding what is rightfully and uniquely mine]." Exodus 20: 3-4 (AMP)

"I can't live without my Starbucks coffee." Idol. "I need money to be happy." Idol. "I need a husband or a wife to complete me." Idol. God is a jealous God. One of his many names is Jealous!

"Do not worship any other god, for the Lord, whose name is Jealous, is a jealous God." Ex 34:14 (NIV)

"For where your treasure is, there your heart will also be." Mt 6:21

Everything you deem important; everywhere you spend your time and money, be it work, the gym, shopping, is where you are placing your treasure. God wants all of your heart. He wants you to depend on Him for everything. God wanted all of my heart, so anything that I held onto, anything I deemed more important than God, or leads me away from God and into sin had to go. And I mean everything.

I had 40 gigs of music at the time. I went through thousands of songs to see if anything was demonic or would open a door. I ended up with 19 gigs. I gave away anything I had in excess: clothes, shoes, books, clothes (I have a habit of buying nice 'clearance' clothes. A lot of what I gave away still had tags on it), sold my desktop computer to someone who really needed it for cheap. Whatever the Lord told me to, I did it.

"Take your clothes to the Dream Shelter in downtown LA."

"Okay, Lord." Done.

"Give this homeless person the pizza you just bought for yourself with your last five dollars."

"Okay, Lord." Done.

"Workout for 18 minutes, not a second more."

"Okay, Lord." Done.

I and the Lord were getting to know one another, and it was great!

CALL TO ACTION:

Are you still on fire for God? How?

_____

_____

_____

_____

_____

If not, why did you stop?

_____

_____

_____

~CHAPTER ELEVEN~

In God We Trust

Wendy: The Rug Got Pulled Out

My sons called and said they had worked on Eric's website and wanted to know when we could come see it. So, I called Eric. He seemed his normal self, but my guard was up right now. This man had just denied me three times to people, saying that," I was just his friend." The day we were supposed to go, again he said, "I will take my own car," so I knew something is still off.

The two-hour drive was hard; my heart was heavy. God spoke to my spirit and said, "Peace I am going to get the glory." As soon as I arrived, my son, James, swooped me up in his arms and held me like a rag doll--the luxury of being 6ft 5. My godson, Chris, came out and hugged me, too, but his face was not happy. I started to walk toward the house, but James nodded at Chris and said, "Mom, let's go for a walk first.

He began to tell me what a great woman I was and that I deserved a king and not to settle for anything less. He said, "I was his hero and always did the best with whatever came my way and that God was well pleased with me." My knees got weak. My son is very prophetic. I knew he was about to tell me something that was not going to be good. He proceeded to tell me that while they were researching sites for Eric and putting in data on him, they discovered that he is involved with not one, but multiple women. I literally fell to my knees and wailed. I could not hold it in any longer. Chris heard me all the way down the street and came running to me. He picked me up off the ground, and they both just held me for what seemed to be an eternity. "God, why? Why can't a man be faithful to me?" God just said, "Peace be still."

My phone rang, and it was Eric trying to get directions to the house. I gave the phone to my son who gave him the directions; then they took me into the house to clean me up. While I was getting cleaned, God spoke to me. "Wendy, this is my son. Please love him past your pain. Have grace for him. I'm not through yet." So, I gathered myself and told God, "Okay, make me brave."

As I came out of the bathroom, Chris spoke words of encouragement over me while James just spoke in tongues. Then there was a knock at the door. Before answering, Chris said, "Mom do not bring this up now, wait on God." So, I got up quickly and went to the bathroom the second time to pray for strength. I quickly whispered, "Lord I forgive him. Please heal my heart".

To be honest, the rest of the day was a blur for me. A few days later, Eric asked to meet with me at my girlfriend's house. He proceeded to confess about another woman and asked if I could forgive him, which I did. Then he shared his heart and said he is trying to wrap his brain around all this, and that it's moving fast. He asked me if we could slow down. I did not even stop to pray I just said, "ok." The next day I got a call from Eric's mother, she gave me: Psalm 105:4-6:

> "Seek the Lord, and his strength: seek his face evermore. Remember his marvelous works that he hath done; his wonders, and the judgments of his mouth; O ye seed of Abraham his servant, ye children of Jacob his chosen."

And --

> "And, ye fathers, provoke not your children to wrath: but bring

them up in the nurture and admonition of the Lord. Servants, be obedient to them that are your masters according to the flesh, with fear and trembling, in singleness of your heart, as unto Christ; Not with eye service, as men-pleaser's; but as the servants of Christ, doing the will of God from the heart."Eph. 6:10-12

But God!

God has righteous anger, and he's not going to let you settle for anything less than what he promises you. God told me, "Get up and go see him. You need to repent for trying to be okay with just being his friend." As hard as it was, I got up and drove to him. He was doing his laundry, and his father called. I ended up talking to him, and he said, " Hi Miss Wendy, trust God's not done with you yet. Be patient with my boy. God always completes that which he started." Boom, there we go that is what I will stand on to give me the strength to say this to him.

"Trust in the Lord with all your heart and lean not on your own understanding." Prv 3:5

Eric finished his phone call, and the laundry and we went back to his house. I proceeded to ask Eric if he was not happy with God's choice for his life? He looked at me confused, so I just repented for trying to be just 'his friend.' I shared with him what God told me, "I'm to be your wife, not your friend. I am not to settle." He said, "I know." He held me for a long time with tears streaming down his face and mine. Then he kissed me on the forehead, then on the lips. My heart's racing. All I wanted to do was love him and be loved by him. God, I want what you promised me. But God...

"Do not stir up love before its time." Song of Solomon 8:4

I caved. Trust I am human. I may be a pastor, an evangelist and all that, but I am also a woman, and I love him with every ounce of my being. Yes, I ended up being with him that night, and in the morning, the Holy Spirit woke me and said, "Okay, repent and leave now." So, I did. I don't even think I got all the way dressed. I cried all the way to the car. "Father, I have failed you." The Lord whispered in my ear, " Shhh, grace I give you, Wendy. You are still my choice for Eric. Now you are not to see him or talk to him for the next three days." I obeyed. I wanted what God had intended for me, and so I was determined to follow God's instructions. Again "obedience is better than sacrifice" (1 Samuel 15:22). So, for the next three days, I prayed, fasted, studied about King David, and stayed in my Word. I got three calls from others who God instructed to war with me.

Sunday came around, and I was supposed to go to church with our bible study group. God said, "Call Eric and ask him to come." So, I did. I even offered to pick him up along the way. God said it was okay, just do not go into his house. So, I obeyed. As we were driving to church, the Lord whispered, "Ask him what his decision is." In my head, I was like, "Okay God, but it's only been three days. God said, "Ask him." So, I did. I asked him if he had made his decision, he said, "No." God said, "Tell him to make it now." So, I did. His response was epic to my soul, He said, "If you are going to force me to make a decision right this minute, if you are in a hurry, don't let me stop you. Go do you"! Wait, what??!

"God, I don't know what you are doing to me, but I can't do this."

God said, "Yes you can. I need you to be strong in me right now."

I went into the church and called the two women coming to meet us. They were stunned as well they had heard God say, "Wendy is to be his wife," as well. John 10:14-18 came flooding in my head. Okay Lord, ok.

"I am the good shepherd, and know my sheep, and am known of mine. As the Father knoweth me, even so know I the Father: and I lay down my life for the sheep. And other sheep I have, which are not of this fold: them also I must bring, and they shall hear my voice;, and there shall be one -fold, and one shepherd. Therefore, doth my Father love me, because I lay down my life, that I might take it again. No man taketh it from me, but I lay it down of myself. I have power to lay it down, and I have power to take it again. This commandment have I received of my Father." Jn 10: 14-18

CALL TO ACTION:

What depths are you willing to go to be obedient to what God is telling you?

_____

_____

_____

_____

~CHAPTER TWELVE~

Serving God No Matter What...

Eric: Breath, Wind & Fire

I had started digging into my Word every day. The Word was filling me up while I was writing a spiritual trilogy that the Lord gave me to write. Wen and I were doing great. The only part of my life that sucked was that I hadn't seen my daughter, who was now 2. I shipped her some gifts every chance I got, but it's not the same as being able to watch her rip open the gifts. But God got me. Keep it moving.

She took me and the bible study group to a Bible-based church in Woodland Hills called In His Presence Church (IHP) with Pastor Mel Ayres and his lovely wife, Pastor Desiree. It was a great service that day. I physically felt the difference between a sermon based on human facts, science, metaphysics, etc.. and one preached from the Bible. Those scriptures during Pastor Mel's sermon stirred up something in me. I was crying during the whole sermon.

Afterwards, we all met outside on the lawn of the church. Wendy turned to the Christian newbies in the group; I included, and said, "Guess what? You guys are getting your prayer language today." What's that? "You're about to find out." She laid her hand on each of our stomachs. A rumble within my spirit began stirring. My arms and legs started tingling. My mouth started muttering, trying to say words, but they weren't words. It was just sounds, syllables, that had a fiery rhythm to them. Wendy said, "Let go. Let it come out." I opened my mouth and gave sound to the quaking from deep inside of me. And right there on the lawn of IHP Church, I started speaking in tongues. Then suddenly, a gust of refreshing wind came out of nowhere and enveloped me. It wasn't windy that day at all. This was unreal. I just stretched my hands out, looked to the heavens and soaked it in.

I said, "Good afternoon, Holy Spirit, my name is Eric.

The Holy Spirit said, "I know. Glad to meet you."

I immediately called my mom and told her I received my prayer language today, and I told her about my lawn experience. She said, "Did you feel the rushing wind come? I said, "yes." She said, "Good. How do you feel? "Drunk." She said, Good." Good doesn't begin to describe how I felt that day. No words can.

"When the day of Pentecost came, they were all together in one place. Suddenly, a sound like the blowing of a violent wind came from heaven and filled the whole house where they were sitting. They saw what seemed to be tongues of fire that separated and came to rest on each of them. All of them were filled with the Holy Spirit and began to speak in other tongues as the Spirit enabled them." Acts 2: 1-4 (NIV)

I now knew what the disciples felt when the Holy Spirit came upon them and introduced himself to them. The Bible was starting to come alive.

Wendy: About My Father's Business

I sat through the entire service and proceeded to pray for people and do whatever God needed me to do. When we were done and headed to the parking lot, I saw tears in Eric's eyes, but he said nothing to me. Nothing at all. God said, "He needs the gift of speaking in tongues right now, and I need you to baptize him in it now." "God, I know I can do all things through you, but is there not one other person that can do this? Really? I am in so much pain." God said, "I asked you, will you do it?"

"Verily, verily, I say unto you, He that believeth on me, the works that I do shall he do also; and greater works than these shall he do; because I go unto my Father. And whatsoever ye shall ask in my name, that will I do, that the Father may be glorified in the Son. If ye shall ask anything in my name, I will do it." Jn 14: 12-14

"Withhold not good from them to whom it is due when it is in the power of thine hand to do it. Say not unto thy neighbour, Go, and come again, and tomorrow I will give; when thou hast it by thee. Devise not evil against thy neighbour, seeing he dwelleth securely by thee. Strive not with a man without cause, if he have done thee no harm. Envy thou, not the oppressor, and choose none of his ways. For the froward is abomination to the Lord: but his secret is with the righteous. The curse of the Lord is in the house of the wicked: but he blesseth the habitation of the just. Surely he scorneth the scorners: but he giveth grace unto the lowly. The wise shall inherit glory: but shame shall be the promotion of fools." Prv 3: 27-35

So I asked everyone from our bible study to get in a circle and began to pray. Then I asked Eric if he had asked God for the gift of speaking in tongues? He said, "Yes," and then began to cry. Everyone gathered around him as I prayed for God to fill Eric up right now. The power of God was so strong, I immediately forgot all my own pain and began interceding for one of my father's children to receive the infilling of the Holy Spirit. What a privilege and an honor. Eric fell to his knees, and his spirit began speaking in tongues.

Lesson: *We are HIS. When we sign up to be all in, to be kingdom builders, His will must supersede your own.*

CALL TO ACTION:

When did you receive your prayer language? Describe the event.

_____

_____

_____

_____

_____

_____

If you haven't received your prayer language, are you saved? No? Then say this prayer:

Lord God,

I want you in my life. I need to know you. I need a relationship with you. Be my Lord. Be my savior. Forgive me for all of my sins. Thank you for sending your only begotten son, Jesus Christ, to die on the cross for me and resurrecting him. From this day forward, Jesus Christ is the Lord of my life. Forever and ever. Amen.

Rejoice!!, you are now a child of God! Can you hear the angels clapping in heaven for you?

~CHAPTER THIRTEEN~

The Day Of Reckoning

Eric: Time to Pay The Piper

"He who covers his sins will not prosper, But whoever confesses and forsakes them will have mercy." Prv 28:13

I remember walking into Wendy's friend's house where we had bible study. Wendy was alone and sitting on the couch. I sat down next to her. By the troubled look on my face, she knew something good wasn't about to come out of my mouth. Weeks before, I had told her that I wanted to slow down because so much was happening. She was my pastor, spiritual mentor, and girlfriend. I'm literally bearing my soul to her, and it started to scare me. So I put the brakes on it. It was hurtful, but it had to be done. So there I am, sitting beside her. She said matter-of-factly, "So?" I took a deep breath and just came out with it. "I have a girlfriend."

Those were the hardest words I've ever had to say to anybody, but I had to do it. The Holy Spirit convicted me in the days leading up to this day, and anyone who's been convicted by The Holy Spirit knows, He won't stop until you confess your sin. He overwhelms you with it until you can't take it anymore. That's where He had me. I had to do it to keep my sanity. The world says it's 'your conscience,' for me, it's The Holy Spirit.

Wendy was devastated, and it was all my fault. She didn't deserve that. I felt like a complete a--. Why would I do that? Now I'm just like every other guy. A playa. Well the Lord doesn't like his ambassadors to be playa's, so I'm going to have to face this demon face-to-face. We didn't talk for days after that. I wanted to call her, but I knew I needed to give her her space to process things and decide if she wanted to be around me anymore. Then I got a call from her about an event going on at IHP. Her voice was cold, devoid of any emotion. Jim Calviezal, who played Jesus in "The Passion of The Christ," was speaking at IHP and she wanted the bible study group to go. I'm in. She picked me up in her egg-white Chrysler 300, and onward we went. On the way, it was noticeably different. The tension was thick. We exchanged pleasantries. I gave her a CD I made for her, surface stuff. Then she looked at me with that 'let's cut the crap' look and said, "So, what's it going to be?"

I said, "I don't know. I need time". This isn't easy. It's an inner battle between the old Eric vs The new Eric. Old Eric is of the flesh. New Eric is alive in the spirit. This was my 'fork in the road' moment. Then those fateful words that changed the trajectory of our relationship came out of her mouth. "Let me know 'cuz I got s--- to do." I saw that neck moving, and she put that extra emphasis on "s--- to do." That woke the sleeping lion. I'm like, "Did you just give me an ultimatum?" "Yes," she said. I saw red. I'm the wrong person to give an ultimatum to, and so without thinking, I said, "Do you." In the silence that ensued, I continued the conversation in my head. "Don't you ever give me an ultimatum. I ain't no California dude. I am a Leo. I don't need you. I am not that dude."

We attended the event. Afterwards, she drove me home in silence. When she parked the car, she said, "Okay well, I release you back to God and repent for being with you. Please do the same so God can use us separately. I said, "No," because I knew this was for real done now. I thought that was the last I was ever going to see of Wendy Darline, and I was okay with that. Or was I? Little did I know that the weeks to follow God would require of me to go and do things for her, and even to continue my relationship with her son, James. Really, God? Really?

Wendy: Betrayed And Scared

When we were done at the event, we drove back to his place so I could drop him off. God whispered, "Trust me," but the woman could not forget that he just said, "Go do you." That was enough for me. We cried for a long time as we said goodbye, He would not repent for being with me sexually, and he would not release me back to God. He just kept saying, "I need time." I prayed a blessing over him and said, "Eric, this is God calling on you, not me, so you have to talk to him about all that." My heart was broken into a million little pieces. I truly loved him. I know what God told me, yet Eric was choosing to walk away, and not just from me, but from the true calling on his life. This was the hardest thing to know that this man was being handpicked by God and did not get it. I said goodbye and drove off, never expecting to see him ever again. However, God had other ideas.

I was broken. I truly loved him with all my heart, but I knew

God needed to be with him. God would not allow my spirit to settle for 'friends with benefits,' or now even just friends. He truly had become my best friend. But God. On my way home God gave me, Philippians 4:6:

> *"Be careful for nothing; but in everything by prayer and supplication with thanksgiving let your requests be made known unto God."*

Revelation:

I was not checking in with Eric on what he, in fact, was being told to do by God. So I did not realize, ladies, Eric had not paid the price for ministry yet. I had, so it was flowing out of my oil. But I was the only one getting the oil. I would have known had I just listened to God and controlled my flesh. I knew Eric was not yet ready. He needed to press in with God first. I could tell by his face he did not want to hurt me, and that he too was in pain, but he did not count the cost of my oil. What I know now is that when you have already been a servant and a wife, it comes naturally to give and to nurture. If you have been a Christian for any length of time, you may also have been practicing being a Proverbs 31 woman. So again, you love God, and you please Him, but now you are giving this man everything before he and God had "the talk," before that man really understood the gift of you from God. Better yet, he didn't yet know how loved and valuable he was to God. Only God knows the man's heart and if that man has counted the cost (Luke 14:28-30).

Ladies, we must trust in God even if he gave you a word about a man, wait for the rest of it.' It's all about "the timing."

"Give not that which is holy unto the dogs, neither cast ye your pearls before swine, lest they trample them under their feet, and turn again and rend you." Mt 7:6

"I charge you, O daughters of Jerusalem, that ye stir not up, nor awake my love, until she pleases..." SOS 8:4

Let's go even a bit further in the book of Ruth. God shows us in detail how to walk it out by faith without knowing the outcome. Ruth kept her eyes on God, trusted wise council from Naomi and worked with what she could while waiting on God to orchestrate the rest. And by doing this, when the blessings came, she didn't just become greedy or self-absorbed, she gave her first born to Naomi. She was able to bring restoration to an entire bloodline. "Obedience is always better than sacrifice." I was to blame. Also, I gave into my flesh. Eric and I were so attracted to each other and had so many encounters with God; we got carried away. We can't blame that on God, but at the time, I did.

Revelation:

I was acting as a wife and giving myself to Eric as if he were my husband. I forgot the rituals of courtship. I was so trusting, not that trust is a bad thing, but sometimes when you think you are trusting God you are really just assuming, you did not wait on Him sometimes you get too eager that you just run on ahead. Have you ever wondered why God never gives you the whole plan? For this very reason right here, God knows what is around the corner, you don't. He knows how to counter-attack the enemy in ways you may not. This is what led me to easily become prey for the enemy to swoop in and throw a flag on the play. I gave my oil too soon. (Mt 25:1-13). I also stopped checking in with God and got ahead of myself. I started acting like his wife, I made Eric my husband before he really was. God had said he was my husband, but I still needed to go through the steps. (God's timing)

> *"Fixing our eyes on Jesus, the pioneer, and perfecter of faith. For the joy set before him, he endured the cross, scorning its shame, and sat down at the right hand of the throne of God." Hebrews 12:2*

ACTION:

It is okay if you realize that you may have gone ahead of the Lord, then stop, take a minute right now and pray this prayer out loud to yourself:

Glorious Father,

"I am checking in. May my footsteps be in perfect alignment with your will for my life right now. Please remove anything that I may be doing to displease you, that you did not call me to do right now. I thank you, Lord, in advance for your perfect timing and your patience with me to make sure I finish my race successfully, In Jesus' marvelous Name. Amen".

> *"The King's heart is in the hand of the Lord, like the rivers of water, He turns it wherever He wishes. Every way of a Man is right in his own eyes, But the Lord weighs the hearts. To do righteousness and justice is more acceptable to the Lord than sacrifice."Prv 21:1-3 (NKJV)*

Does this mean Eric was not really the one? No, not at all, however, we must stay in touch with God and let HIM lead, guide and direct you every step of the way. I believe now in hindsight that it is important in any relationship that you establish boundaries, tighten your sphere as well as sweeping out your past, realizing that marriage is now going to be your first ministry. As you begin to do ministry seemingly things or people are no big deal are the very weapons Satan will use to sabotage the work, so keep your peace, relax, remember that you are a gift and let God lead you both.

> *"Houses and wealth are inherited from parents, but a prudent wife is from the Lord." Prv 19:14*

> *"He who finds a wife finds what is good and receives favor from*

the Lord." Prv 18:22

"A wife of noble character who can find? She is worth far more than rubies." Prv 31:10

"She is more precious than rubies, nothing you desire can compare with her." Prv 31:15

CALL TO ACTION:

How have you discerned that Satan is trying to destroy your life?

_____

_____

_____

_____

_____

What steps have you taken to block his attack on you and your marriage? What scriptures are you standing on to stop him?

~CHAPTER FOURTEEN~

Heart Breaker

Eric: The Painful Revelation

But God wasn't through with me. He was burning off the dross. He was making me face something I didn't want to. And that was I can be devious, manipulating, flattering, cunning. All traits of flesh. All traits of Satan.

> "But I am afraid that just as Eve was deceived by the serpent's cunning, your minds may somehow be led astray from your sincere and pure devotion to Christ." 2 Cor 11:3

> "With cunning, they conspire against your people; they plot against those you cherish." Ps 83:3

cun·nin - adjective
1. having or showing skill in achieving one's ends by deceit or evasion.
Synonyms: Sly, scheming, devious, crafty, wily.

Wily?? Where have I seen that word before?

> "Finally, my brethren, be strong in the Lord and in the power of His might. Put on the whole armor of God, that you may be able to stand against the wiles of the devil..." Eph 6: 10-11

If I am to work for God, I can't be manipulative, cunning or deceitful.

These are weapons of Satan. So I repented on the spot once I got this revelation:

> "Wash away all my iniquity and cleanse from my sin...
> ... Cleanse me with hyssop, and I will be clean;
> wash me, and I will be whiter than snow...
> ... Create in me a pure heart, O God,
> and renew a steadfast spirit within me.
> Do not cast me from your presence
> or take your Holy Spirit from me.
> 1Restore to me the joy of your salvation
> and grant me a willing spirit, to sustain me."
> Ps 51: 2,7, 10-12

And the Lord answered:

> "I will cleanse you from all the sin you have committed against me and will forgive all your sins of rebellion against me."
> Jer 33:8

And here I thought the stripping was done with the clothes and such. No,

He stripped me down to my bare bones.

After that, he started bringing revelations about my character flaws to the forefront. I had to face the unsavory things about myself and the collateral damage it's doing to the people I eventually end up hurting. Those women are his daughters. I've been hurting and breaking the hearts of God's daughters. That revelation alone brought me to my knees. I didn't do this to just one of his daughters; I did it to almost every girlfriend I've ever had. And it happened almost like clockwork. I would start to emotionally shut down in my current relationship due to three reasons, I lost my attraction to them, I was bored, or I was not being heard. Once I reached those stages, I would start looking for a new relationship, but I wouldn't end my current relationship. Eventually, they'd collide and explode into some ugly event. The Lord showed me that I've been doing this since college! I'm 48 as I'm writing this.

And it's not the girls' fault because I didn't say anything. I just went on about my business and became a functional boyfriend counting the days until I was out. So unfair. So unmanly. So punkish. It was time for me to face myself and the hard truth. I was a dawg. A nice, charming dawg, but a dawg nonetheless. I'm not the abusive type of dawg, nor the domineering "women serve me type dawg, nor the "I'm god's gift to women" type. I'm worse. I'm the one who gains your trust, then breaks it. This was a hard pill to swallow. Where did this come from? How did I come into agreement with this behavior?

My father didn't raise my brothers like this or me, nor did he think this was manly or cool by any stretch. The men I grew up around were not play-as. They took care of their families and home. If you were cheating on your spouse on the side, they'd shun you. When my dad found out I was messing with two women, he said, "To me, it looks like you can't make a decision." That's not a compliment. That's a knock against my character as a man. So I begged the Lord, "Help me to uproot this flaw from my heart." And he showed me its inception.

Quick Detour:

When I was about 7 or 8, my second oldest brother, Bill, had a sassy little friend named Sheryl. She was a boisterous, fun-loving type girls. The day I met her, she looked at me and said, "You have the prettiest eyes, little Eric. Oh, those girls are going to be in trouble when you grow up. You are going to be a heart-breaker."

heart·breaker - noun
1. *a person who is very attractive but who is irresponsible in emotional relationships.*

Irresponsible in emotional relationships?? Hmm, kinda fits doesn't it? Be very careful of the names you call your children. They just may prove you right.

> *"Death and life are in the power of the tongue, And those who love it will eat its fruit." Prv 18:21*

Now I'm not sitting here blaming her for saying that. She was being nice, but that somehow sank into my being and stuck. How do I know that you ask? I'm writing about it 40 years later. Of all the things said to me over my life, I'm remembering this moment.

It was time to own up to it. I had already told Wendy, but I hadn't told the woman. A year and a half already passed since Wendy and I had ended our thing, so I thought I was Scot-free, no need to bring it all back up. Ehhh – wrong answer.

> *"For there is nothing hidden which will not be revealed, nor has anything been kept secret but that it should come to light."*
> *Mk 4:22 (NIV)*

I made the drive down to her. When she saw my face, she knew I had something bad to tell her. I sat her on the bed... and divulged my sin. She was as angry and hurt and heartbroken as you'd expect. All I could think of as I watched her go through all of these emotions was, "I'm a horrible person. Nobody deserves this." As she wiped the torrent of tears away, I said, "I'm really really sorry," and headed for the door. She said with a trembling voice, "Where are you going?" She wanted to work it out. Whoa. Now I really feel like crap.

CALL TO ACTION:

What revelation did you get about yourself from Eric's testimony? Are you a heartbreaker?

_____

_____

_____

_____

_____

_____

Is there a role model that you modeled how you deal with the opposite sex in relationships? What did you observe from them?

_____

_____

_____

_____

_____

_____

Are you copying how they behaved irresponsibly in your past relationships? If so, how are you going to change your actions in your present relationship? What scriptures are your foundation for the new 'God-you?'

_____

_____

_____

_____

_____

~CHAPTER FIFTEEN~

The Walking Dead

Eric: Roaming The Desert

Life just wasn't the same, not being able to talk or see Wendy. We had that thing you can't fake. That heart-skipping-a-beat thing. And now without her, my heart was barely beating. But I got this, "you win some, lose some," and all those idiotic maxims that never meant anything until you go through something came to my mind.

During the next six years, I continued my relationship with the women. I talked to Wendy maybe once on the phone during this time. The Lord would still use her to give me scripture. I would wake up some mornings and see a scripture or a chapter to read, or a link to a YouTube sermon in my email from her. And they would always be about something I was going through in my life at the time. All I could do was shake my head and wonder if I made a mistake. Did I let my ego and pride cause me to cancel God's plan for my life?

Those questions wracked my brain many nights over the coming years. When you are having supernatural experiences left and right, and then they suddenly stop for years, you definitely start questioning your choices. The fact that Wendy kept being obedient to God in regards to me was astounding. That takes a strong woman to do that. I don't know if I could do that if the tables were turned.

I often thought about the last time we met in person. It was at a burger place near her job, and she proceeded to speak into my life, about what my trilogy was going to do for the kingdom, the divine appointments I would have with A-list producers. As we were wrapping up, she looked me in my eyes with a stern glare and said, "Beware of women hitting on you. They're not really attracted to you; they're attracted to 'the anointing' God gave you." Pow! What a punch to my ego. "Well thanks a lot," I said sarcastically. "Glad to know I'm not attractive without God's "anointing." Great. It became hard to take prophetic words from her after that because I didn't really know if it was coming from God or her broken/scorned heart. But again, it was all my fault. I brought this on myself. If I would've been a righteous man, I would not have taken either of these women through this.

Wendy: Hardened Heart

Well, here it goes. This will probably be the hardest part to tell. I plan on being transparent. Trust me, none of this is to brag, condone or justify bad behavior or sin but to expose the devil's plan so that you can stop, turn around and run back into the arms of your King. His grace alone is sufficient. I faithfully served God for so many years; I was sure that I had it together in the area of temptation and that I would be able to withstand the flaming missiles of the enemy.

Remember that I said after church God still used me to baptize Eric with the Holy Spirit, well I know now that was God trying to keep me in alignment with him and his promises so that I would not surrender to my flesh and do something to sabotage this moment. He also was trying to keep us connected. But my flesh was strong at that moment driving home from Eric's house, even after an amazing time in the Lord at church, and being used by God to bring the baptism of tongues to one of His. This warrior took off her armor, threw it in the back seat of her car, and drove up the 14 freeway blaring my secular music. I began to be enraged, hurt, and sick all the same time. I literally felt my heart break into a million tiny pieces. The enemy's flooding me with the memories of my failed 23-year marriage to a man who not only had affairs, but that reminded me continuously that he never loved me at all, that he only married me because he had to.

The anger and the fear overwhelmed me to the point that I no longer could even see the road, tears burning down my face, heart racing, the girl in me screamed, "No more"!!! I pulled the car over to the outlook and as I got out the car. I shouted to God, "No more!" God spoke to me in the softest of a whisper, "Trust Me; I got this under control. Please wait." I said, "Oh no God, I cannot be the discarded one anymore. Why Is it so easy for them to always discard me? What is wrong with me?"

{Hindsight: This is where I opened the door for the enemy to come in like a flood.}

"God," I begged at this point, "please choose someone else. I have no fight left in me. I can't do this. I have no fight left whatsoever." The pain was so bad at this point; all I could do is wail uncontrollable sobs. An officer saw me there at 2 am, crying, fallen to my knees. He got out of his car, came over and picked me up, and just held me until I could calm down enough to tell him I was okay. The officer gave me his card and said to call him anytime and that he would keep me in his prayers. "Don't lose hope," was the last thing I heard him say. I got back in my car, wiped my face. Calmly began to pray and just said, "God, I love you, but I thought you were going to protect my heart. I need you to take this pain, I need you to take back this promise, and I need you to take this mantle. I cannot do this anymore".

Quick Detour:
What you don't know is up to this point I already had overcome a slew of things. I was born with birth defect, had an abusive childhood, teen pregnancy, abusive marriage, attempted suicide, miscarriage, burying my second child, multiple battles with cancer, and other major health issues. My first born had cancer twice. I've endured character assassination from the church and church alienation. But over the past 25 years, I've also had to walk through multiple miraculous healings. Each time I was getting

stronger in the Lord, knowing God was for me. So It wasn't like I was a wimp, I just had enough in mind, body, and spirit. I had thought since my ex-husband wasn't a believer a lot of the infidelity and abuse had more to do with him than me. Eric was different. He was a promise from God. So I let my guard down.

Revelation:

The three things I did wrong which contributed to that night's meltdown:

A. I was mad at myself because I had given into premarital sex

B. I forgot that the enemy was going to up his game because we were both Christians.

C. I was isolated.

This is the revelation I have now, but not then. Then I was too focused on the pain, the rejection, the fear that is all too familiar to me. This was my first time walking through feelings of a man's love. "God, why didn't you protect me from this?" From that day on, I allowed my heart to harden from hurt. It was subtle, but it was deliberate. Hope deferred makes the heart sick is a real thing.

> "Hope deferred makes the heart sick, BUT a dream fulfilled is a tree of life." Prv 13:12

TAKE ACTION:

If you think things should look a certain way or happen in a certain time, pray this right now.

Father,

Your ways are not my ways your time is not my time, so I will trust in you and lean not on my own understanding, in Jesus' mighty name. Amen and Amen

If you get nothing else out of my story I pray this right here will bless you.

So, I have given God back my mantel. What is a mantel you may ask? For me, the mantel was my calling. However, I had forgotten it was also my authority. For every battle I had won over the years, I had increased in knowledge, wisdom, power, authority. So, for the next few years, I did not have the mantel or all those components in this area in my life. I still loved God, I still walked the best I could in my walk as a believer, but I no longer saw myself as a warrior, pastor, evangelist, teacher, prophet, etc... I just saw broken, discarded and hurt.

I knew this was not just us; it was my family. It was all the people in our Bible study that were hurting as well. Over the next 11 months, every person had to go through a negative experience, including my Mom, who loved him so much and had gotten her hands healed after Eric prayed for her, lost hope and the infection in her hands returned for another year. My son had a hard time trusting any man that tried to come into our lives. Our friend, Daphne, lost her battle to cancer. Was it all directly our fault? Maybe not, but we must always remember we are a body, and when part of the body is not functioning correctly it affects the whole body.

So trust me, the rest was easy for the enemy because I walked out from under my covering and to victim road. I was there for the picking. Dating men that not only did not know God, but they also would never know me. Broken attracts broken. So I was being cheated on, lied to, and surrendering my hope for whatever came my way. I even tried to get married, not once but twice! Both times though God would not let it happen. That's grace and mercy. When you can't see him, trust me, he is still there. He's letting you figure things out. He's giving you the space to grow. Grow in being sick and tired of doing it my way, that is.

"His word is true, He will never leave you nor forsake you." Heb 13:5

Not talking to GOD was starting to wear me down, so after about 2 years of this, I reached out to Him. And He was right there waiting for me. He was literally right there in my car! I found myself back at that lookout point and I said, "God, I am sorry. I have no idea how it got this way, but I love you." God in his most gentle whisper said, "Do you trust me?" I was totally raw with him and said, "I want to." I heard God say, "I will take it." God softened my heart once again.

That afternoon, I got a call from Eric. I just looked up to the ceiling and mouthed, 'Really?' He proceeded to ask how I was? So much pain flooded me because I never stopped loving him. However, I just said, "Oh I am great." The biggest lie ever. All I wanted him to do was say 'I am sorry' right then, but he didn't. So I quickly got off the phone. I still loved him; nothing could change that because God put that love there. I looked up to God and said, "That was the best I could do." God said "That's okay. Trust me." I just nodded and under my breath said, "I am trying."

CALL TO ACTION:

Are you a victim of doing things your way instead of God's way? If so, how?

_____

_____

_____

_____

_____

What things/opportunities have you gained from doing things your way?

_____
_____
_____
_____
_____
_____

What things/opportunities have you lost not doing it God's way?

_____
_____
_____
_____

~CHAPTER SIXTEEN~

Free At Last

Eric: Jesus Take The Wheel!

During this time, my daughter, now 2, and her mom moved from Chicago to Arizona. Now instead of having to go 2500 miles to see my daughter, I could drive 5 hours to Lake Havasu, AZ. Thank you, Jesus! We were on speaking terms as my daughter's third birthday rolled around. I finally got to see my beautiful daughter open up Christmas gifts in person. She loved her gifts as all two-year-old's do, especially a lion teddy bear from Wendy. My daughter loved that bear. Oh, what a joy. She's full of personality so watching the faces she made was worth all the times I didn't see her. The day went along perfect.

The night was an entirely different story. I booked a hotel because I couldn't stay at her mom's house. She had two teen boys before me, so what example would that be setting for them? When all of the Christmas festivities were over, I was saying my goodbyes to my daughter, telling her I can't wait to see her tomorrow. Suddenly, her mom had a fit. "Why didn't you give that money to me? "It's $30! I just spent $150 on her along with bringing diapers, wipes, etc.." There was some more back and forth, then I left and went to the hotel, anxious to see my daughter tomorrow.

The next day, I pulled into the driveway and noticed the gift I bought for my daughter's mom from my parents was sitting outside by the door. I walked up to the door, picked up the package, and then rang the doorbell. I saw my daughter running toward me through their glass front door with a big smile on her face and her arms out ready for a great big hug from me. She was yelling, "Daddy" as she was running toward the door. But suddenly out of nowhere, her mom swooped her up, said, "Nope," and took her back to her room and locked the door. I never saw my daughter again that trip. I was burning inside, but I knew I couldn't do anything stupid. Black man. In Arizona. From California. And it was her home. The odds are not in my favor. So I hopped in my car, gassed up, and started the 5-hour trip back to LA. While heading, back I needed to talk to somebody to calm me down, so you guessed it, I called Wendy. She said to come to her house so we can talk, so I did. Hours later, I arrived at her apartment. I recounted the events of the last 36 hours to Wendy. She listened with a caring heart, then said,

"Have you broken your soul tie with her?"

Que?

"Soul tie. Everybody you have ever had sex with, you form a soul tie."

"Can't say that I have."

"The Lord told me to walk you through that today."

"Now?"

"Yep."

(sigh) "Okay."

Fellas, imagine having to name everybody you ever had sex with. Now imagine having to state your list to the hottest girl you've ever met. Awkward. But if that's what the Lord needs me to do, let's go. And I proceeded to name the names. If you could have seen the look on Wendy's face, trying to be pastoral, but she's a woman, too. Nobody likes to hear about your ex-partner's partners. But we made it through in one piece. I think. Yet I still could not bring myself to break one with her. The fact that God used Wendy to do these things for me even after everything I had done, was a testimony to her walk.

CALL TO ACTION:

Have you broken soul ties with your exes/one-night stands/flings/hookups? If not, make a list of everybody you fornicated (had sex with outside of marriage) with.

_____

_____

_____

_____

_____

Once you have the list, say this:

Lord God,

I ask for your forgiveness for fornicating outside of marriage. It is a sin against you, Jesus and the Holy Spirit. I will honor your commands, laws, and precepts and treat my body like the temple of the Holy Spirit that it is. (Say your name) I forgive you. I know better, and I will do better.

In Jesus' Name, Amen.

Next, say this prayer for each name on the list::

Lord,

I ask that you forgive me for creating an unhealthy soul tie with (person's name). I give them back to you and ask that you would cancel the soul tie. Forgive me of any offense, sin, or lie that I committed against them. I ask that you make them whole, bless them and help them find the perfect mate you created for them.

In Jesus' Name, Amen

Don't be surprised if you are emotionally-spent, yet feel like a huge burden has been lifted off of you after doing this exercise. You never realized you were carrying around all of your past relationships into your new relationships... that is until now.

~CHAPTER SEVENTEEN~

Picking Up The Pieces

Wendy: Repentance Is Key

Six months later of God wooing me, I was back into my word and putting my ducks in a row. I began to fast. I prayed for God to break soul ties with Eric and me and for God to bless his life and to create a new life for me. God's words were so tangible to me during that fast I will never forget it. God said, "I can not break that soul tie, but I will walk you through your healing." "Oh okay." So I began to really focus on God. God would give me words of knowledge. He would use me to lead others to him. Even though I still felt broken, God still had things for me to do.

During this time, I got really sick again. The doctors were not sure what was going on with me. Determined to walk all this out, I pulled up my big girl panties and started cutting out friendships and other things that were not healthy for me. I got back on point with my eating, exercise, and my prayer life. I prayed in tongues two and three times a day. I had already lost the bulk of my "saved" friends after the divorce, but the few I had, we started a bible study at my home. I was so focused. Again God spoke to me about Eric. He spoke to me about the prodigal son. I could not and would not call him, but I would pray in tongues for him.

One night after work a few months later, I got really sick, throwing up, dizzy to the point of falling in the bathroom and hitting my head. I was on the floor until the next morning. One of my girlfriends suggested I come and live with her so that I would have help when I needed it. So I moved in with her and was working 50 hours a week. I was fighting something, yet, the doctors, as usual, were puzzled. This is nothing new with my history. I just kept my eyes on God, still not being perfect. Still giving in to loneliness at times, always justifying that I was just trying to "move on." But God would always remind me of Eric, of our encounters. Then I ended another relationship. When I ended this one, I had been getting prayer from a Pastor friend of a friend, who was praying with me and giving me scriptures to read. I was trying to have some accountability.

I surrendered myself to God again and was determined to be celibate and really give God everything in my life. I even told God I had forgiven Eric because he popped into my head at that moment. God asked, "Do you trust me for everything?" I said, "Yes, you can turn my mantel back on." I heard God laugh. I'm sure he hadn't turned it off, but I had no other way of expressing myself. Again just being raw with you all. I loved serving God. I loved being His warrior, but then the one time I asked him for something--after much prodding on his end mind you--I get hurt and disappointed. I just wanted to go back to the way things used to be, but God said: "NO, we are doing this new thing." God would remind me all the time that what He says, goes. That he is faithful. I would always answer, "God, yes you are." But Eric has free will. To that God said, "Yes, he does. He has the free will to choose my life for him or his own version, watch and see". I thought, Oh God, I am sorry. I am not trying to limit you." I never said that to God again.

A lot of time would go by between hearing from Eric, yet God was obviously doing something because he would show up in my dreams, or he would text me or email me or call. I just did not have faith in Eric to really get who I was. I stopped believing that his love for me existed based on his actions and what I could see.

Eric: Checking In

I hadn't heard from nor talked to Wendy in 2 or 3 years now. I was trying to move on with my life and stay on the up-and-up. I'm still living in LA and driving down to the woman's house every week. I'm planted at IHP Church. I'm in the men ministry, prayer ministry, parables ministry (which is writing sketches to go along with the pastor's sermon). I'm helping with the food pantry ministry (giving food and clothes to the homeless); I'm working the camera at Sunday services. I'm all in for the Lord. After one Sunday service, I saw Wendy's friend whose apartment we used to have the Bible study at. We say hello and I ask,

"How's Wendy.

"She's fine." She's living at the beach now."

I'm like "What? Of all places? How crazy is that?"

I sent Wendy an email after I received one of those LinkedIn connection requests. She said she didn't send it. Hmmm, then who did? As we caught up, she said she was doing great. She was now a licensed life coach. She was writing and ready to publish her children books, and she now owns a semi-pro football team. Wow, I said, you're rolling along, aren't you? "Yep." "Good, I'm glad to see you prospering." But I wasn't "glad." Happy, but not glad. That meant she didn't need me. That day, she officially became the "one that got away."

The conversation continued. We both apologized for things that God was bringing revelation to us about each other, and we came out of agreement with some things that were miss communicated and misunderstood. Again, she spoke about my scripts selling and commercials I was going to get and the 5-fold ministry, blah-blah-blah. When your life is stuck in a rut, you don't want to receive "your amazing future in God." I need some help right now, or I won't be around in the future. We agreed to do a 3-day fast so we could press into what else God had for us. That ended the next day for some reason I don't fully remember.

CALL TO ACTION:

Did you and your spouse have a miss communication about something that sent both of you off on separate paths? What was it?

_____

_____

_____

_____

_____

_____

Now that you recognize it, have you acknowledged the other person's side of the story? If you haven't, what would you tell them now that you wished you would've said then?

_____

_____

_____

_____

_____

~CHAPTER EIGHTEEN~

Dying In The Wilderness

Wendy: Trusting My Process And God

Part of that new thing was for me to have an expectation, to be his bride, to have desires and know that he would meet them. That was hard for me. Again Eric reached out to me, but he always started the conversation or text off with, "God told me to contact you," but then would follow it up with, "Do you have a Word for me?" Oh, that would just make me mad all over again. "Just apologize!," I would scream in my head, but never say to him. I always felt like he wanted his cake and me too. So I would just say, "No," and then not respond any further. He would not push it past that. "I'm fine," would be my only reply when he would contact me over the next several years, with fresh tears burning my face every time.

Since he never elaborated, I felt strongly that door was officially closed. So I would ask God for revelation on my life. I would ask for fresh perspective. I would pray for strength to not fall into temptation. God started to use me again to minister. I was getting invitations to speak at women events sharing my own struggles and encourage others.

So now the enemy knew he would have to be a lot more creative, so my Pastor that I was being accountable to had called me that he would be in town and wanted to meet up with me to discuss with me about helping at one of his churches. I was excited and began praying for direction. Meanwhile, God again says, "Do you trust me? I said, "Yes." The next week, on my birthday, I got a call from my boss on my day off that they had to lay me off. It was a nationwide company layoff. I said, "Okay," knowing God must be calling me into full-time ministry.

So the following week, this Pastor comes to town. I follow him around to different churches and meet all these people, but something was just not right in my spirit. I wasn't sure what it was. I prophesied over people, prayed for people. It was so liberating. See this was my heart's desire. But after being "dis-ordained for divorce," I had not really thought about being a Pastor in a church. I was trying to walk out what I thought was this new thing God kept talking to me about.

After a week of following this Pastor around, he calls me in for a meeting to discuss something. We met, and he began speaking into me about my calling, my mantle, saying all the right words. This went on for a while. Then he says, "God told me you're to be my wife and I want to take care of you." Wait, WHAT??! I was in such shock; I just sat there with my mouth wide open. When the meeting was over, I just shook his hand, said goodbye, and drove off. I got halfway home when I heard God say, "You never answered HIM." I pulled the car over; I said, "God, do you want me to marry this man?" God said, "Text him this, "God's will be done." So I did, but God what about the ... (I paused) God says, "Yes?" "Never mind." Every time I was with another man, the pictures of Eric and the prophetic words would all come rushing in like a flood. Once God's done something, everything else fails in comparison. However, the enemy knows your weak spots, which is why you must work on them daily and keep your guard up at all times. Yes, even in church. I would pray for Eric in tongues always as he popped into my heart. That way I would never be involved in praying my will, but God's, always.

Eric: The Suddenly Of God

I was in a bad place. A very bad, dark place. I had to move in with the woman because I was evicted from my apartment in LA. I didn't want to, but nothing else came through at the time. God had supernaturally paid my rent the last few months. One time, in particular, blew me away. A court-agreed upon payment was due to my landlord on Monday. On Saturday, I didn't have a dime. I mean not a dime. I just had a few food stamp dollars left. As I was washing dishes, God said, "Be at the church on Sunday." "I'll be there," I said as I rinsed the dishes.

I rode the bus to church that Sunday my car was impounded for expired tags. I go to IHP for the 9 am service, nothing out of the ordinary happened. I went to the 11 am service. Nothing happened. I stayed for the 1 pm service. Again, nothing happened. I went to a writer's ministry meeting until 3 pm. Again, nothing. As I headed out of the church, nobody was out there waiting for me. "Oh well, I guess that was a false alarm." As I exited the church to head back to the bus stop, the writer's ministry leader called out, "Eric, hold on a second." I stopped. She came up to me reaching in her purse. She handed me a folded piece of paper. She said, "God told me to give you this." I opened the folded paper, and it was a personal check from her for $750! The amount of my rent. I just crumbled on the ground in tears. I couldn't believe it. God showed up for me! God cared for me! God provided for me!

A couple of weeks later on a Saturday, another miracle happened. After a men's ministry session with Pastor Mel at IHP, he had us break off into smaller groups to pray for each other. In my group, a man asked for prayer regarding a woman he and his wife had taken in who was addicted to drugs. He was heartbroken for her, so we prayed. As others were praying, The Holy Spirit came on me. By the time it was my turn to pray for the man, I was on fire. The Holy Spirit-led prayer brought the man to tears. Then He told me to do what Paul did in the Bible.

"Now God worked unusual miracles by the hands of Paul, so that even handkerchiefs or aprons were brought from his body to the sick, and the diseases left them and the evil spirits went out of them." Acts 19:11-12

Without thinking, I asked if somebody had a handkerchief or a napkin. Nobody had one. The man said, "I have a pen." I grabbed it and had everybody put their hands on it as I prayed another Holy Spirit-led prayer. Afterwards, the man left with the pen. The following Wednesday night service at IHP, the man came over to me as I entered the church. I noticed he was with a bright-eyed young girl whom I had never seen before. His eyes were filled with love and awe. He gave me a warm hug, then introduced the young lady to me. At the end of his introduction, he said, "This is the young lady we prayed for on Saturday. And she is 4 days sober." Tears streamed down my face. A miracle just happened. And then the young lady chimed in, "You were the one who prayed over the pen?" "The group did," I said. She reached in her purse, brought out the pen and said, "I haven't let this pen out of my sight since Saturday. I eat, sleep, and shower with it." I just smiled through the tears streaming down my face and gave her a big hug. Wow, God, wow! I watched her give her life to the Lord, be water-baptized, and blossom in her new drug-free life at IHP. God is an awesome God!

I was thriving while barely surviving. God allowed me to witness more signs and wonders in the coming weeks. My faith was growing by leaps and bounds! That is until another court-appointed payment came due weeks later that November. I was standing on the scripture,

"The Lord shall supply all of my needs according to his riches in glory in Christ Jesus." Phi 4:19

Then the 11th hour came... and no money miraculously appeared. I was waiting for another miracle, some secret angel to knock on my door with the rent check. Nothing. "What happened Lord? I don't understand." The one thing I did understand; I would be evicted. I had to get out. I told Pastor Mel my situation, and he counseled me on what to do. "No shacking up unless you're married." He said. "It's God's way or no way." I didn't take his advice. When D-Day came in January, and nothing and no lodging situation transpired, I caved and went down to live with the woman.

That was a gut punch to my spirit. I felt like I was ripped out of the spirit-filled IHP church and planted by the beach. That wasn't a good trade-off for me. I thrive on sunlight and creative energy. I came from New York to LA. New York's creative energy is off the charts. LA's creative energy is about half of New York's. San Diego is half of LA. You get my point? I did what I could to maintain my LA routines: I religiously watched IHP online every Sunday and Wednesday. Read more chapters. Walked while praying in the morning. In fact, I never unpacked my stuff in because I was determined I was going back in a month's time. I stopped fornicating.

The sunny beach life felt like the wilderness to me, and I was dying from thirst, fast. I was on a dark, slippery slope. Life became tedious. I couldn't write. I didn't feel like being around anyone, including the woman and her family anymore. I just sat around watching TV bored out of my mind. I started watching dark crime shows: First 48, Forensic Files, Hoarders, and other fear-focused shows. I never watched those shows before. But now, they're my comfort food.

> *"Be sober, be vigilant; because your adversary the devil walks about like a roaring lion seeking whom he may devour…" 1 Ptr 5:8*

Dark thoughts began to swirl in my head. "You could end it all, and the pain would go away"… "But what about my daughter? My parents? God? He spoke to me in an audible voice. Was it all for naught?" I didn't hear much from the Lord while I was by the beach. I began to wonder, "Was heaven closed? Is God disappointed with me because I chose the path I chose?

I'm desperate with no one to turn to. I decided to do something I hadn't done in three years, call Wendy. I have to find out what is going on in the spirit realm. I called her, and we talked for almost three hours. She did the same things she always did: prayed with me, gave me scriptures to stand on, and chapters to read. She left me in a better place than when we started the conversation. I felt I could go on. I felt God was somehow still there, but he was coming through her. And suddenly, my life force kicked back on from within.

All of that time I spent walking and talking to God, reading my bible and memorizing scriptures came back with a vengeance. I said, "No, God will never leave me, nor forsake. I am the head and not the tail. I'm from above and not beneath. I'm blessed and highly favored. Fearfully and wonderfully made. No weapon formed against me shall prosper... They just kept pouring out of my spirit until I was back in my right mind.

"So then faith comes by hearing and hearing by the Word of God."
Rom 10:17

On September 1, 2015, during my God time in the morning, I prayed and then said to the Lord, like Samuel did, "Speak Lord, your servant is listening." Isaiah 61 flashed through my mind and echoed in my ears. He said, "Stay in this chapter for the next year." And I did. I started to fight back. Getting healthy, reading my word daily, praying in tongues. I started getting out of the house and writing at a local college library. There was some energy there, and I could work without being distracted because nobody knew me. My creativity came back in droves. I felt alive again. The woman I lived with who wasn't into the church thing, all these years, started to want to go to church, so I went with her. I wasn't feeling it. Let me put it this way, once you've been part of a spirit-filled church, it's hard to settle for 'just going to church.'

While I was working at the library one night, my dad called me with an urgent message. I quickly called him back because my dad doesn't make urgent calls. He told me he was standing with a cousin of mine who used to work for the NBA who has a script that needs to be written. I eventually talked to my cousin, and he gave me the job of writing the script. It was the first paid writing job I had in a while, and it gave me a surge of energy. I wrote that script in 30 days. It just flowed like it used to back in LA. After I finished that script, I continued working on others. I got an agent. I had producers shopping my scripts. I was back in the zone. Life was good. As the summer started, I was above water and happy. This year is gonna be my year to get back to LA and finish what I started.

I got two calls from back in MD from my nephews. They were going through growing pains, and I wanted to help them since I hadn't been there for them in their teen years. After they each told me about their woes, I begin telling them about Jesus. Who he is and why you need him. I told them, "We're Ingram's, God is in our

DNA. Our ancestors started churches, freed slaves, all with the help of the Lord. They all lived from the Bible." All of this starts coming out of me like a sermon. I'm on the library balcony pacing like I'm preaching. I led them both to the Lord. I called my parents, and they were both ecstatic. And then my dad says, "Eric, you are stepping into your destiny and purpose." Evangelist (check). Prophet (check). 2 down, 3 to go.

CALL TO ACTION:

What prophecies have been spoken over you?

_____

_____

_____

_____

_____

_____

Are you pressing in with God to find out what you need to be doing in order to align yourself with his destiny for you? If so, explain.

_____

_____

_____

_____

Eric & Wendy Darline Ingram

~CHAPTER NINETEEN~

Pressing In For The Truth

Wendy: God Confirms A Second Time

My second trip to Redding, California came in July 2012. It's true; God is a faithful God. He is not a man that he should lie. He has been so gracious, so very gracious and good to me. My life is truly blessed now that He is in it. This was how I felt as I left Friday morning for Redding. There was a cool chill in the air, and I was eager to make my way up to Bethel Church to have some much need communion with my King. I love him so much, and I so enjoy the corporate worship that happens up there. So much love fills the atmosphere.

Five hours into the drive, my friend, Cathy, and I decided to stop in Sacramento for some walking around time and food. I stumbled upon a wedding store, and the Holy Spirit told me to go on in. Inside, there was a lady, and she said she had been waiting for me. I tried on two dresses. They were so beautiful. Little did I know this would be the beginning of my journey with God this next week. His theme was preparing me to be and receive as a bride.

Saturday morning, I began to prepare to receive whatever my King had prepared for me. I listened to worship music and just bawled all the way to the church. Once inside, I began soaking in the sanctuary, I just leaned back in my seat and closed my eyes. I had no idea what was about to happen next. Three people came up to talk to me they had Australian accents and were very young. They said God told them to find me and to bless me like the Three Wise Men sent for Jesus.

The first young man told me, "You are God's faithful one. You have given in and out of lack and abundance. This is your time to receive. God will supply all your needs. This is a season of rest and restoration."

The young woman chimed in, "God is the creator of heaven and earth, and all that dwells. He is painting his masterpiece in you. I see him with vibrant colors painting you a new uterus, ovaries, Fallopian tubes. God's going to give you a son, wait no twins!"

The second man, "God said he has served satan notice. He has tried and failed and is no longer allowed to touch you or your camp. He must return everything. Many gifts are coming to you in the next several months. Just continue to rest and be at peace, that which you have sewn shall reap a great harvest."

The first young man spoke again, "God did bring this King (Eric) to share your life with. He can be trusted with your gift,s, your heart, and has great faith to believe for these desires for you."

"WAIT,WHAT??! We have been apart for years," I protested in my head.

This brought me great happiness and much weeping. A desire I had long abandoned, but my King didn't.!!!

Lastly, the young lady whispered in my ear: "You are not selfish, it's your time!"

The next two weeks, I avoided the Pastors texts. I just would pray and give him to God. Three weeks later I got a call from him. I proceeded to tell him my calling and what God promised me. Dumb move on my part! I just gave this man the blueprint to my heart!

"Beware of false prophets, which come to you in sheep's clothing, but inwardly they are ravening wolves." Mt 7:15

I got sick again, only this time much worse, I had a stroke. I became weak and vulnerable which he used as his opportunity to swoop right in and be the "hero" saving me, protecting me, and walking out the word for healing. *However*, over the course of the next two years, I was pursued, manipulated, and abused by this man. Yes, he may call himself a pastor, and yes, God may use him at some point, but what I experienced was not GOD! Yes, I gave into his pursuit and thought I would marry him. But God. Every time something didn't feel right, and I brought it to his attention he would use the Word to manipulate and control me and physically and emotionally abuse me.

Was God speaking to me in this time? I was so sick. I had had a stroke and was now dealing with cancer and a tumor on my brain. They finally discovered I had Hashimoto's disease which was causing 90 percent of my problems. They had me on at least five drugs. I was just trying to survive at this point. My son, an adult now, had moved me in with his wife and began speaking the Word over me. Yes, I was still with the Pastor, and yes, he moved right in with us.

This went on for a while, but once I got healthy, I said, "God, if this is not of you, please remove him and forgive me." Later that week, he moved out. And wouldn't you know it, Eric called me the same day. We talked for four hours. I shared everything with him. I was honest, raw, very vulnerable, and so was he about all he had been through. We agreed to fast and pray for God to show us the way to go forward. He agreed to fast for a week and call me back. HE NEVER DID! The feelings of rejection flooded my being once again. This took me down a spiral turn of feeling rejected, and sickness came flooding back in.

You would think that was enough, but no, I again was under attack. My health worsened, and the Pastor convinced me to take him back. Why might you ask? Because in that moment of weakness of feeling like you are never going to beat your illness, no one else wants you. Satan reminded me that this man wants you; he's not like your first husband who abandoned you when you were sick. He is not like Eric, who prays with you and then just disappears on you. Notice I say satan reminded me of that, NOT God. But at the time that I was fighting so many demons, I thought it was God speaking to me. The other thing is narcissistic people are very good at being charming, charismatic, saying what you want to hear. Notice I said telling you what you think you want to hear, NOT what you need to hear.

Well, it only lasted a few weeks this time. Thank you, God, for stepping in and starting to expose things. As I started reading my Word, focusing on God's love for me and not on the condition of my body, I could see more clearly and was able to break up with that Pastor. To find out not only was he living a double life, but he was also doing it with the help of his fellow Pastors at his church. So I took this to the Baptist board, forgave him and never looked back. And that's when Eric emailed me and said, "Did you hear my name in the spirit?" I began to sob. I cried out to God. "I know God you have grace for all I have done, but is this still your will? Why does Eric always call me right when I pray? Your will be done. What can I do about this? Is he asking about me? Does he want the life you chose for us?" God said, "From this day forward, you Wendy Darline, keep it 100 with Eric. No matter what or how he acts, be 100, with your heart, mind, and spirit."

Over the next several weeks, the Lord instructed me on what to pray for and what to stand on. As I opened my Bible, the paper with the list about my husband from the beach fell out. A flood of emotion came over me. God told me to grab a small bottle that I had on my dresser and put my tears in there. I told God right then, "I surrender all for your perfect will to be done for me." Later that day, I got a call from my best friend, Bethany, in Alaska. She was getting ready to get married and wanted to talk to me about what God had shown her. She proceeded to tell me that she had been praying for me and asking God why has Wendy not found her husband, and yet you are allowing me to get married? The Lord told her because Wendy refuses to settle for anything less than what I already promised her. She told me, "God is going to bring your husband to you. Not just a husband, but *your predestined husband*, your promise because you refuse to settle for just anything!" Bethany knew Eric, and she knew Eric was who God had shown me. This gave me the strength to keep going. Over the next few weeks, the Lord had me add oils of frankincense and myrrh and cinnamon, hyssop, gardenia and a few other oils and told me this would be my wedding oil. Every time God gave me a word to stand on, I knew I was believing for my victory, for my promise!

My girlfriend, Noelle, who is an amazing worshiper, asked me to come live with her. God told her to take care of me and to flood me with the Word and worship. She said she felt I was like Esther being prepared as a bride for the King. During the next several weeks, I forgave myself finally, really forgave myself for my mistakes and said, "God, even if you never heal me again, I will never stop praising you." And that alone was hard because I still had days when I couldn't speak or use my left side of my body from both the stroke and the Hashimoto's disease. Some days I could not get out of bed, but my girlfriend would just put the music on, and I would close my eyes and praise him inside. She spoke,

> "I shall not die, but live, and declare the works of the Lord." Ps 118: 17

It took about 6 months of trusting God, worshiping and soaking, to finally feel like I could function somewhat again. I got rid of every friend or guy from my past (except for Eric, God would not allow me to block him). I cleaned out Facebook, blocked people and started to really gain strength in saying "No" to others and saying "Yes" to being alone with no expectations of the future. Then, Eric contacted me again only I gave a different response, God said tell him to just pray for you, so I did. But God... He knew how to bring healing. God said when he contacts you again just ask me what to reply back. My trust became in God again and not what Eric did or did not do according to my ideas.

I started seeing some new doctors, and they were able to help me get on track. And God showed up and did his part in healing me from the tumor on my pituitary to the tumor on my thyroid. My mind and my thoughts were aligned with God's word daily because the enemy was relentless at trying to remind me of failures, rejection, etc... But *I choose* what to think on.

"Whatever things are pure, lovely and of good report." Phil 4:8 Reminding myself of who I am in Christ, really receiving and forgiving myself. I loved myself back to life.

One day, I sat straight up in bed and so, "Okay Lord, I believe you for my promise, so please heal my body, so my husband gets a whole and healthy wife ready to serve with him. I started being able to work out. I started being able to process food again and to help my son a little at the office. I started to be able to see my pep coming back. I no longer looked to the past, I just focused on my new beginnings. My heart was so full of God again. We had been through so much together. Oh, how I love God he truly is the love of my life. I am madly in love with him more than ever!

Eric and I just remained friends, best friends and as far as I was concerned. That would be enough, for now. I was able to stop expecting him to get on board. I was so focused on God that my grace for Eric was bountiful. I had a dream he had to go home; I asked him if everything was okay? He said everyone was fine and I let it go. Yet God woke me in the middle of the night and asked me to pray for Eric's mom and dad, so I got out of bed, fell to my knees and just prayed in tongues. My heart was heavy, but I knew God chose me to intercede for something big. So I emailed Eric and then just went back to sleep.

CALL TO ACTION:

What revelation did you get about your ex from this chapter?

_____

_____

_____

~CHAPTER TWENTY~

The Circle Of Life

Eric: My Fathers In Heaven

On August 3, 2016, I woke up and checked my phone as always to see what happened in the world while I was sleeping. But this day was different. I saw that my mom called me at 5:30 am PST, that's 8:30 EST her time. That's not normal. I was on a script deadline, so I decided to get dressed, head over to the library, get set up, then call her back. Once there, I went outside the library to call her back. Something wasn't sitting well. My mom answers in her normal sweet voice, "Hello." Hi, what's going on?" "Dad had a stroke this morning. We're on our way to Southern Maryland hospital." "Okay," I said, still reeling from hearing the word 'stroke.'

Quick Detour:

My family has been blessed with great health by the grace of the Lord. In my entire life, the only 'medical emergencies' in my family have been my dad having to take high blood pressure medicine, and my mom was in a serious car accident when I was a sophomore in college. That's pretty much it. So a stroke is way out the ordinary.

"Who's with you?," I inquired.

"Junior (my brother)." We have to go. We're here."

"Okay, let me know what's happening. I'll be on the next plane if need be."

I couldn't do any work that day. I kept my phone by my side all day. No calls. I called my sister at work for an update. She didn't even know. She said I'll get back to you. Minutes turned into hours. Day turned to night and still no answer. All I could think was, "God, come on now, not my dad."

I messaged Wendy to pray for my dad in the hospital. She said.

"Praying. Everything's going to be fine." I went home in a daze of worry and anxiousness. I couldn't sleep that night. All I kept saying was, "Not my dad, Lord." The next morning, I get a text from Bill, my other brother, that simply says, "Get here asap." I book the earliest flight that I possibly can, the red-eye back to DC. I arrive in the morning. Bill picks me up from the airport, drives me to my mom's house where everybody's gathering. We load up the cars and head up to MedStar Hospital near Howard University in NW, DC, to their Stroke Unit. My heart is pounding. I've never been in this situation before. Ingram's don't do hospitals. God has protected our family.

We make the walk from the garage through the maze of hallways to get to the stroke unit. It was literally the longest walk of my life. It was one of those 'Poltergeist' hallways that seemed to get longer and longer the more we walked. They buzz us into the unit. We pass people in different stages of distress. I walk into my dad's room. There he is, asleep, a tube in his throat. Breathing machine aspirating. Skin glistening. He's just asleep. He would continue to sleep for the next six days.

The crew of doctors that received him took us into the room that Thursday and said they wanted to pull the plug Friday. The problem was my dad was what they call, "locked." No blood was circulating to and from his brain. He had the worst stroke humanly possible in the worst place humanly possible. The basal artery is in the back of your head at the base of your skull. It's where the four arteries meet to circulate blood to and from the brain. Well, all four arteries were blocked at the basal artery. No blood is going anywhere in his brain. So his body and organs started to shut down. They went around to each of my family members and answered whatever questions we had. When it got to me, I said, "What's the hurry? It's been less than 48 hours. Why this Friday deadline? They said he's not going to improve or come out of it. They've done all they could do. I said, "Fine, but he's in God's hands now. It's not over." My mother stayed in her word. She told me Friday morning that she got a word from the Lord as she was doing her morning reading.

> "Blessed are those who have regard for the weak;
> the Lord delivers them in times of trouble.
> The Lord protects and preserves them—
> they are counted among the blessed in the land—
> he does not give them over to the desire of their foes.
> The Lord sustains them on their sickbed
> and restores them from their bed of illness." Ps 41:2-3

I stood on it with her. As we were driving to the hospital, it finally hit me. This was the purpose I was home. To bring my father back from the dead. A modern day miracle is going to happen in the Ingram home. When we went back, I talked to him like he was alive and well. I read the bible to him. Played scriptures in his ear from my phone. Anointed his head and feet with oil. Prayed in tongues. Waiting for Jehovah Rapha to show these doctors who's the true healer. Because of that scripture, my mother refused to pull the plug that day. We're going to see what the weekend brings.

Friday night, as I was sleeping, I had a dream. In it, my dad came to me in a pristine white robe, his normal charismatic self. He looked at me and said, "You got it." I knew what that meant, but I wasn't receiving it. I am here to witness a miracle by Almighty God. That's the devil playing tricks on me. I will stand and stand firm on the word of God. My dad will live and not die. The weekend came and passed. Monday came and passed. The new team of doctors planned to pull the plug on Tuesday if there was no progress, but my mom said, "it's not time." She told them, tomorrow.

Tomorrow came. August 10th. As we arrived, the entire new team of doctors ushered us into the same waiting room as before. Over the last few days, I had seen them usher other families into the room, and when they came out, the families were usually in tears. Now it was our turn. They spoke about what's going to happen and how his body's going to react when they take the breathing tube out. It'll look like he's moving, but it's his body's involuntary movements, the lead female doctor said. "It'll look like he's struggling breathing. It's his lungs taking their last pumps. I'm not listening to any of this. All I kept saying was Jeremiah 17:14, "The Lord said he is healed, so he is healed," over and over again. "By his stripes, you are healed (Is 54:10)". "He sent out his word and healed them; he rescued them from the grave (Ps 107: 20)."

We head into my dad's room. We each go around the room and say what's on our heart. The phone rings. It's my daughter. She's 8 now. I told her mom about my dad, so she has something to tell him. She tells him, Granddad, I love you, and I want you to get better." Luckily, they spent a weekend together January of that year. It was the first time they spent time together since she was one-year-old. For 7 years, he never saw his granddaughter. 7 years. Keep me focused, Lord.

The nurse removes the breathing tube at 3:53 pm. Now it's my turn to talk. I already anointed his head and feet, and now I say, "In the name of Jesus, get up and walk, dad." I just keep saying it over and over. His breathing becomes labored. "Come on, dad, come on. In the name of Jesus, get up and walk."

His chest heaved its last breath. A pop came from his mouth; then an eerie stillness came over the room as his chest deflated. I looked at the clock. 3:59 pm. It finally hit my mother as she started to wail. My sister, nephews, and cousins left the room in disbelief. I stood there in shock but still talking, "Wake up, dad. Wake up." Then suddenly, a burst of sunlight broke through the cloudy malaise outside the window. That was it. My dad passed over. Wendy was the first person I texted. She texted back, "I'm sorry. You did a good job. God is so proud of you." "For what?," I answered. My dad died. The torment followed. Was it because I didn't have enough faith? Should I have come on Wednesday instead of Thursday? I kissed his forehead, told him I loved him, you and I know he's still with me. No tears. Not because I was being tough, it's because I know he's with God now. Why cry about that?

We ambled to the car and gathered around as a family. My mom said, "Eric where do you want to go eat for your birthday? I said, "The last place me and Dad ate when I was home last, the American Café." Happy birthday to me.

CALL TO ACTION:

What life event jolted you so deeply, it made you seek God like never before?

_____
_____
_____
_____
_____
_____

How did he begin to heal your insufferable pain?

_____
_____
_____
_____
_____

~CHAPTER TWENTY-ONE~

Friends Helping Friends

Wendy: Revelation In A Storm

I got the email that his father was ill and he was flying home. I began to pray. I began talking to God about why he shows me things he doesn't show Eric. God spoke to me and said I have a different relationship with you that took you almost 30 years to develop.

The reason I chose you for Eric was so he could know me the way you do. I knew you could love him enough to get him to see me the way you do, to feel me the way you do and that he would inherit all these gift's I placed in you. Pray for his pride and his heart right now so it stays soft while his father will pass. I wept for what seemed like two days, just interceding and then I fasted because even though Eric wasn't with me, God's perfect will still needed to be done. God increased my love for him. He started showing me that Eric, too, had been just as miserable without me as I had been without him. Only this time it was okay. This time I knew my calling and higher purpose in God and so that took precedence over my personal need. This time I would wait on God. God is faithful. His word does not return to him void. He is the same yesterday, today, and tomorrow.

> "God is not a man, that he should lie; neither the son of man, that he should repent: hath he said, and shall he not do it? or hath he spoken, and shall he not make it good?" Num 23:19

> "And being fully persuaded that, what he had promised, he was able also to perform." Rom 4:21

So during the holidays Eric emailed me, and we spoke on the phone for the first time, but God would only let us speak on certain things.

I let him know that I was waiting on God's promises for my life, that's it, and that's all. Whatever they may be. He said the same.

We realized it had been 7 years since God spoke to us and showed us each other. That night as I went to sleep, God for the first time allowed me to remember all the things God had showed me, all the things God did with Eric and I, and the memories didn't hurt anymore. They were real, the whole thing was God, but we let counterfeit people, hurt, distractions as well as some ego get in the way of God's perfect love affair.

Eric: My Fathers' Favorite

I ended up staying with my mom in Maryland for the next 8 months. She and my dad are very able bodied people, but now she's alone. They were together for 60 years. My dad left a humongous hole. He lived such a full life. Here's a Facebook post I wrote when he retired in 2012 from the government:

"I just want to give a loving and resounding applause to my dad who retired recently from his job after 53 years of hard work and service. I feel I'm the luckiest son of Earth because I have the two greatest Fathers watching over me, The Lord God Jehovah and GI, Sr.. He is my brightest example of what a man is and supposed to be. He sacrificed over and over for me and my siblings and taught us about all forms of love: The tough love, the never give up when things weren't going our way love, the open my house to help my family love; the how to be married for fifty years to my mom love, and the find what you love to do and do it all out love. He's strong yet humble. A jokester who doesn't tolerate BS. A man of God who serves The Lord and all who walk in his path. Hard-handed with a soft heart. He knows how to give of himself and take time for himself. He stands for what he believes with no apologies. He puts his family (extended included) and others before himself. He's one of the few who will stand in the face of adversity when others will flee, crumble, or just give in/up. My dad is the American and Dream:

-Overcame a tumultuous childhood

-All State HS quarterback

-Married his college sweetheart

-Served our country in Vietnam

-Traveled the world

-Raised four strong, independent kids

-Homeowner

-Got his kids through college

-Received his college degree at 57

-Celebrated 50+ years of marriage to my mom

-Retired after 53 years of service in great health (I honestly don't remember him ever calling out sick growing up. Ever!)

-Has the same best friends from his twenties

-Five grandchildren

-The family patriarch who still sings in the church choir

I can go and on about the life lessons and wisdom he imparted to me. He's the greatest man I know. And proud and honored to be his son is the greatest understatement ever. A nugget of wisdom he once told me was, "A man/father never gets his props until later (in life) after everyone sees he was right." Well dad, I'm here to tell you, YOU WERE RIGHT... I love you and congratulations good and faithful servant, job well done.

Your loving (and best ;)) son,

EI

My dad lived the American Dream. Lived it. It's such an honor to be his son!

Wendy and I started talking more and more. She was always a source of comfort for me. This was a pivotal time in my life. I had to decide how I am going to live the rest of it? Death brings clarity like nobody's business. As the pallbearers from the United States Air Force carried my dad's casket to his burial place in Arlington

National Cemetery in Virginia, this scripture came to mind:

"You have made my days a mere handbreadth; the span of my years is as nothing before you. Everyone is but a breath, even those who seem secure." Ps 39:5

As the 21-gun salute echoed throughout the cemetery, my mortality engulfed me. Time waits for no one. Death is batting .1000. And one day, it's coming for me. How can I stand before God knowing I haven't done the things he put inside me to do? Jer.1:5

"... I have made you a prophet to the nations."

Time to make a change. I have to be about my father's business no matter who gets hurt or offended. Call me what you want, but one thing you will not call me is a disappointment or a slacker to God. I prayed and talked to God and asked Him to forgive me for slacking and to please help me get back on track.

I was still in a funk for a few more months. I finally got a taste of what grieving is or felt like. It just comes on you out of nowhere. I'd be fine, laughing and joking with my mom or siblings, then pow!, I'd look at a pair of my father's shoes or smell a whiff of his cologne and then realize, he's gone. He's passed over. He's in heaven. What's he doing now? Is he watching us? Was he ready to go? Did he see a white light? I should've called him more. I stumble upon old pictures of us I'd never seen (he was notorious for taking pictures but never getting them developed). As I scanned through the photos, I realized what I'd given up chasing my Hollywood dreams: time with my parents, friends, family, my daughter. The devil got me. Gladys Knight's "Midnight Train to Georgia" came to mind. In that song, she sings about a fame-seeking entertainer having to catch the train back home because he couldn't make it big in LA. I heard the devil laughing. Gotcha. I was hurt.

Quick Detour:

You ever notice that right before somebody makes it big or they just made it big, they have a family tragedy that wrecks them. It's usually the person who supported them the most. I used to look at that as a bad thing. Now I understand it's the process of life. In order for the young ones to grow, the older ones must move on. It won't happen unless the older one dies. It happens in movies all the time, right?

In the coming days, Wendy started talking to me about a father's inheritance in the Bible: Joseph, Jacob & Esau, and I started to see, to understand, it was time. Time for me to become who God ordained me to be. My dad's words echoed in my head from my dream, "You got it."

"When I was a child, I talked like a child, I thought like a child, I reasoned like a child. When I became a man, I put the ways of childhood behind me." 1 Cor 13:11

Revelation:

As I read this scripture, a revelation just hit me. Why is this verse in this chapter about love? Because it's time to become mature in love and put away my childish antics in the love realm.

Two weeks after burying my father, I was doing my morning prayers when my Dad barged into the conversation with God and me and just started ranting about how proud he was of me and he heard and felt everything I did for him at the hospital. I got my pen and began scrawling down everything he said. One of the things he said stood out more than the rest to me. He said, "Marry Wendy." Wow, that's out of the blue. He never met her. He talked to her on the phone one time. But that's what he said clear as day.

The following month, I was driving my mother to run errands. As we drove around, a God moment happened. I would play gospel music on the radio or we'd listen to Joel Olsteen. This time we were playing the radio and this song came on the radio. The chorus was, "You're running, You're running from your calling." Those words gut-punched my spirit. A seed was being planted in my heart. The rest of the song spoke about God is calling. Just say yes. We arrived at our destination and did our business. About an hour later, we got back in the car. I started it up, and bam, the song starts playing from the spot when I got out of the car. I'm like what?? Did the DJ stop the record until we got back in the car? He had to. We listened to the rest of the song on the way home. I realize the song was talking to me. From that day on, almost every time I was in the car, the song came on. God was sending me a message. Eric, you're running from your calling." I told Wendy what was happening and she said, Eric, have you accepted your mantle?" "Um, I don't remember the actual acceptance part. I just started living for him, but never formally accepted it. "Well are you ready?" ... ...

"Then he said to them all: "Whoever wants to be my disciple must deny themselves and take up their cross daily and follow me." Mt 16:24

Yep, I'm ready. And on that day in October 2016, seven years after hearing the audible voice of God, I accepted my mantle that the Lord designed for me from the beginning of days. Wendy has always been the one to take me through the next step. As our first Thanksgiving without my dad was coming upon, I was miserable.

God was pressing me about the last big hurdle. The last idol I had. Whatever God asks you to give up and you have to think twice about is an idol!

> *"Thou shalt not have any false gods before thee." Ex 20:3*

And I knew what idol he was talking about. The woman by the beach. I'm tired of going around this mountain Lord. Help me. "Take this cup from me, but nevertheless..." I searched the bible for a situation to help me on what to do. The story of Abraham and Isaac came to mind (Gen 22). It was time to make a decision. I talked to Wendy every day. She filled me with The Word. She inspired me. Encouraged me to become who God already said, I already was in the kingdom. I couldn't really talk spiritual stuff with the other woman. And that was a big problem. God was calling me to a spirit life and she didn't want any parts of it. Time to man up.

> *"He who loves father or mother more than Me is not worthy of Me. And he who loves son or daughter more than Me is not worthy of Me. And he who does not take his cross and follow after Me is not worthy of Me. He who finds his life will lose it, and he who loses his life for My sake will find it." Mk 10: 37-39 (NKJV)*

The person was not so much the idol, but the "free will", and trying to keep some portion of my old life was. God is very clear you cannot pour new wine into an old wine-skin. Now I get it!

> *"Neither do men put new wine into old bottles: else the bottles break, and the wine runneth out, and the bottles perish: but they put new wine into new bottles, and both are preserved."* Mt 9:17(KJV)

I chose Jesus, and I chose Wendy!!!. A gargantuan weight was lifted off my head. A soothing peace came over me. I had to make Jesus the priority in my life. And I finally realized I needed Wendy to help me do that. So I made the call. I felt horrible almost to the point of throwing up after making that call. Again, nobody deserves this mess I created. As I was laying on the bed feeling like a piece of trash, I noticed the time and date on my phone. 9:17, November 8, 2016. Whoa! Seriously? November 8th??? You have got to be kidding me! November 8th was the day I met Wendy 7 years ago. 8 is the number of new beginnings. Come on God, are you serious??... I cried myself to sleep that night. God is so faithful.

As December roared in, the lingering effects of our first Thanksgiving without dad was still in the air. Now it was the first Christmas. This year was the first time I was home for Thanksgiving or Christmas in 16 years. I was either in New York or LA and would always be out of money during the holidays. And now I'm home and my dad's gone. Arrrgghhhh!

During morning prayer, I read an email devotional that talked about Issachar's anointing for times and seasons (1Chr 12:32). As I read the article, God said, "Read that part again." I read it again. He said, "Again." Issachar was known for having the anointing for knowing the times and seasons. God said, "I am giving you this anointing today. Hold out your hands." I held out my hands and bowed my head. Suddenly, a tingling sensation went from the top of my head down to my arms and fingers, then down to my legs.

Days later, I and my family celebrated our first Christmas without my dad. It was a little somber as to be expected but was still gratifying for me since this was my first Christmas with them in 16 years. As we cleaned up the wrapping paper, I just felt like I had a huge hole in my heart. I was looking forward to 2016 leaving. It was an earth-shattering year, both good and bad. It was the year I had to put on my 'big boy pants.'

CALL TO ACTION:

How did you heal from the heartbreaks you endured from the past?

_____

_____

_____

_____

_____

~CHAPTER TWENTY-TWO~

Year Of Restoration

Wendy: It is On!

The beginning of the New Year I had a triple hiatal hernia repair and continued seeking God for healing me in my mind, body, and spirit. Eric and a group of women prayed for me. Eric was online, not in person. He was still in Maryland. When we finished praying, one of the young ladies asked Eric how do you know Wendy? So he told her the story of how we met. As he did, I saw the old spark in his eye and heard the love in his voice like we used to be. My girlfriend, who had arranged our first meeting, began to cry and pray in tongues. The young lady who had asked Eric the question became filled with love and the spirit of God, and she said to Eric, "No wonder your prayer was so full of love, power, and might." Who knew then that God, the God of restoration, was birthing in us something life-changing that would literally set us back to the beginning.

"And I will restore to you the years that the locust hath eaten, the cankerworm, and the caterpillar, and the palmerworm, my great army which I sent among you." Joel 2:25

After my surgery, God came in my room and flooded me with love and power and said, "Your healing is now, and we are in acceleration mode!" He gave me 1 Kings 19 to read.
(Please read it now before continuing. We'll wait.)... . ...

Eric called daily to check on my progress, and by February, we were praying and talking regularly. There was a shift, but neither of us was talking about it. We both were being conscious of our words and keeping God at the front of our intentions and speech. Absolutely no talk of love or anything personal, just all God.

Eric: Holy Spirit, Help!

I was starting to get back to being myself: being funny,

laughing, writing. The dark cloud from my father's untimely death started to lift just in time for the coming spring. Funny how that happens. Wendy and I were talking every day until this one day; we had a dust-up over a text she sent me I felt was a smack in my face. I felt so offended; I didn't talk to her for the next two weeks. I didn't have time for silly drama. I had been in a dark place for months. I'm not going back there over some false accusation of something I didn't do.

About a week into the dispute, on a Saturday night, I got a call from Senior Pastor Reggie from my mom's church, New Dimensions Kingdom Ministries in Washington, DC. This church was a Godsend for me. It was a spirit-filled church where they let you ask questions or comment or give words that The Spirit gave you. They wouldn't start until the Holy Spirit said so, and they would end when the Holy Spirit said so. Incredible. They let me lead prayer, prophecy, give words of knowledge. They were letting me step into my walk with no seminary training. Most of the parishioners went to seminary and knew scripture like their names and cell numbers. Not me.

We exchanged pleasantries and he paused dramatically, then said, "Prophet Eric, I'm sorry, I should have called you earlier in the week. The Lord put something on my heart to tell, but I got busy. So I apologize. What the Lord put on my heart this week is... you are supposed to give the sermon in service tomorrow." Speechless, I eked out the words, "Ooo-kay." How in the world am I supposed to give a sermon?? Am I allowed to give a sermon? I'm not a pastor. I didn't go to seminary school. I don't have a clue how to format one. What's my topic? What am I able to speak on, biblically??

Suddenly, an uncommon peace came over me. I knew this was coming in my spirit, so it's really not a big shock. I just didn't know it would be now. After my dad's funeral, I prayed to God that I'll do whatever you need me to do, just take care of my mom." Her dealings with social security, the VA, settling my dad's estate were very taxing in patience and time. Thank God my dad had the foresight to have ninety percent of his affairs in order--and he was working on the last ten percent before he passed--but being with my mom through the rigmarole of claiming her benefits was no walk in the park. So fast forward to now, most of the things she needed had been taken care of so she was straight. So now it was time to hold up my end of the covenant.

{Note: Please don't think me and God 'negotiated' this. It was already a part of His master plan for my life.}

I took a deep breath and answered the pastor, "I'll be ready." I hung up the phone and looked up to the heavens and said, "Okay, here we go. What do you want me to talk about?" There was no answer. I reiterated, "Just tell me what you want me to talk about and I'll get on it." Nothing. I started to panic. I know how to get up on stage and talk, those years of doing stand-up prepared me for that. I was also a motivational speaker so I can give a concise message. But this God. Jesus. The Holy Spirit. You can't fake your way through this. I kept asking for my topic in the coming hours, but still, nothing came. Finally, as I was getting ready for bed, I heard a whisper. "You already have a sermon." Where? I said. "Facebook." What? Oh yeah, I had started a FB page entitled, The Love Movement" a while back where I would write about scriptures about God's love in the Bible. I had about ten sermons (posts) with scriptures and word definitions. I was lead to speak on one of my favorite scriptures from 2 Timothy 1:7:

> *"The Lord did not give me a spirit of fear, but of power, of love, and of a sound mind"*

And,

> *"But when they arrest you, do not worry about what to say or how to say it. At that time, you will be given what to say." Mt 10:19*

I read over it a couple of times and went to bed. I said, God, it's in your hands now.

The next day, we arrived at church. Throughout the ride, I was trying to stay calm. I decided not to tell my mother what's about to happen. I'd rather see the look on her face when the pastor calls me up. We sat in the front row like we usually do and the service commenced with prayer and the reading of the word like we always do. Then it came time for the sermon. Pastor Reggie walked up to the podium and began to tell people "We are in for a treat today." He told them the same story he told me about how he forgot to tell 'this person' they were speaking today, but The Lord made sure today was the day he spoke. "Minister Eric, would you please come give the word today." My mother smirked with surprise as I headed to the podium. I got her good. She looked so proud. This was a good thing. No, this was a God thing.

Those steps up to the podium were the hardest. But once I stepped up on the stage, all those years of stand-up came rushing back. I laid my notes out on the podium, gave thanks to God and asked the Holy Spirit to guide me through this sermon and we were off., Thirty-three minutes later, as I closed up my first sermon, I received "amens" and "that's a good word" from the congregation. The word inspired people thanking God for his unconditional love. It was p.o.w.e.r.f.u.l.

"*And you will be called priests of the Lord, you will be named ministers of our God." Is 61:6*

When I got home, all I wanted to do was call Wendy and tell her, but we were still not speaking. That ruined my high. It was such an empty feeling not to have anyone to share this amazing movement of God with. Especially Wendy. She was the one who God used to start me on this journey. And now at the culmination, on my day of promotion, she was nowhere to be found. That was a very lonely, empty feeling. Another week passed. I figured the Lord would deal with her and that situation. I did what I was supposed to do. Wrong!

"Do not allow your anger cause you to sin; Do not let the sun go down while you are still angry." Eph 4:26

What were my sins? Bitterness. Holding a grudge. Not forgiving an offense. Going to bed while still being angry. Jesus said what, "Forgive your brother 70 x 7." And I didn't forgive Wendy. Once the Holy Spirit convicted me, I repented, and God said, "Call her today." So I did. After we both said our peace, we asked for forgiveness for our behavior. Right after we did that, I got the biggest revelation about Wendy beside God telling me she's my wife seven years ago.

I got the revelation about why things hadn't taken off for me in the last seven years. Why my career was stagnant. Why I wasn't as happy as I could be. Why I felt like I was going through life with my emergency brake on. I'm a V-12 engine, Lord, let me loose. But the reason why things had been 'delayed' was because I was not to do it alone.

> *"And the Lord God said, "It is not good that man should be alone; I will make him ahelper who is just right for him..."Gen 2:18 (NLT)*

When that hit me, tears came to my eyes, and I told Wendy. Now I get it. I had to get rid of the Lone Ranger spirit. Is there anybody in the Bible who did God's work by themselves? No. They had helpers right beside them. Jesus had his disciples. Elijah had Elisha. Moses had Aaron. Paul had Timothy. David had Nathan. And Wendy was my helper. That changed everything. Once I got that, the Lord started to hit the 'acceleration' button.

> *"You ask, "Why?" It is because the Lord is the witness between you and the wife of your youth. You have been unfaithful to her, though she is your partner, the wife of your marriage covenant." Mal 2:14*

CALL TO ACTION:

What revelation did you get about restoration from Eric and Wendy's testimony?

_____

_____

_____

_____

_____

_____

After reading this chapter, what is your revelation regarding the importance of relationships?

_____

_____

_____

_____

_____

~CHAPTER TWENTY-THREE~

The Lone Ranger Strikes Again!

Eric: Whoa Kemo-Sabe!

The Lone Ranger Spirit is not an official name of a spirit. It is more aptly known as prideful spirit. In the world today, there is glory being given for being 'self-made.' "I did it by myself." Not in God's kingdom. Nobody does anything by themselves in the kingdom. Look at how many popular scriptures there are about partners:

"Where two or more gathered in my name, there I am in

the midst." Mt 18:20

"It is not good for man to be alone. I will make him a helper suitable for him." Gen 2:18

"Can two walk together, lest they agree? Amos 3:3

"Two are better than one; because they have a good reward for their labour." Ecc 4:9

"One can send a thousand, but two can send 10,000 to flight." Jos 23:10; Deut 32:30

Look at how many biblical heroes had sidekicks:

- Adam & Eve

- David & Jonathan

- Abraham & Sarah

- Elijah & Elisha

- Jesus & The Disciples

- Paul & Timothy

- Ruth & Naomi

- Esther & Mordecai

The list can go on and on...

    It takes a thousand partners to raise a man of God. Especially someone like myself who didn't catch all of the hints right away. As men, the world raises us up to be Lone Rangers or lone wolves. If you ask for help, you're deemed as weak. If you're not performing super-heroic works every day, you're not considered a man. I got a lot of these teachings from my dad. He was a man's' man. He'd settle whatever problem face to face, forget all that texting and phone calls. face-to-face.

I'll never forget the first time I saw my father cry. It was during Rev. Jesse Jackson's DNC speech in 1984. As he talked about being born and his mother dying during birth, my dad started crying. Later I learned from my mom my dad's mother died giving birth to him. That was one of the greatest gifts my dad gave me, crying. Crying has nothing to do with manhood. It is a human emotion that, for me especially, helps me wash out whatever sorrow or pain I"m going through. Jesus wept. God weeps and wails like a woman in labor. Emotion. Men don't really worship God. We are more worried about how we look. "I ain't worshiping another man." I believe one of my strongest qualities is I don't care what people think. I will cry, weep, get on my knees to worship God, Jesus and The Holy Spirit. No problem.

So this brings me back to the Lone Ranger Spirit. One of the reasons it's so prevalent and honored today is the devil knows we have no power unless we do things God's way. "Sing and pray, go on, don't wait on the Holy Spirit. We got to get everybody home so they won't miss their football games that they could record." We must get back to fellowship. We need help. God ordains help. Not by yourself. Pastors are quitting and getting sick. Why? They're doing everything themselves. And that's where I went off course. I had to do it big. I had to be the top dawg. I wouldn't go see my parents for years at a time because I was chasing the golden carrot. This tunnel vision spilled over into every area of my life.

"My people perish from lack of vision." Prv 29:18

And...

"Don't you know a little bit of yeast ruins the whole batch." Gal 5:9

I couldn't see my way out of anything because I was too prideful to change course. Too stubborn to take direction. Too hard-hearted to surrender my life to God and put every part of it into His hands. I was afraid to ask for help. And I lost, gave up or missed out on so many things that I could never get back. I was blinded by a deep-seated desire to be wildly successful, and then I would come home as a hero and save my family, my town, my people. For the second time, I realized what I'd given up chasing my Hollywood dreams: time with my parents, friends, family, my daughter, and even Wendy. The devil got me again. I heard the devil laughing. Gotcha.

ACTION:

If God can bring this revelation to me, I know He can do the same for you. If you identify with the 'Lone Ranger Spirit.' If it has ruined your life, family, relationships, happiness or any other area of your life, stop... and pray this prayer with me.

Dear Father in Heaven,

Forgive me of all of my sins. Father, I forgive those who have hurt or sinned against me and caused me to come into agreement with the spirit of self-reliance and self-preservation. I pull that root up and all other roots attached to it (such as selfishness, callousness, narcissism) right now in Jesus name and I cancel those hurts and ask that Your love come into those hurt places in my heart and heal my brokenness. Holy Spirit, convict me from this moment forward if that lone ranger spirit rises anywhere within me. Lord I now ask that anyone I hurt in the process of being self-reliant, anyone that I may have hurt, neglected or rejected because of that spirit of lone ranger, I ask that you heal their hearts and give me an opportunity to make it right with them. Thank you for hearing my prayers. Thank you for keeping me in times when I didn't deserve it. You are the God of Heaven and Earth. You are the Holy Redeemer and the Healer of Broken Hearts. I am healed. I am delivered. I am sanctified by the blood of Jesus.

In Jesus name, Amen

Now go make two lists: one for the people who hurt you and another for the ones who have been hurt by you. Forgive those who hurt you and pray for God to bless them. Now take the list of the ones who were hurt by you. Pray for each one of them. Call them if you're able to. If you're not able to, write a letter to them. Go with a contrite heart and realize you hurt them. So if they won't talk to you, that's fine. But you have to make the first move and God will do the rest.

CALL TO ACTION:

Have you been bound by the 'Lone Ranger' spirit?

_____

_____

_____

What has this spirit stolen from you? Your life? Your relationships?

_____

_____

_____

_____

_____

Declare and Decree the Word of God over this part of your life right now and every day for the next fourteen days:

" I will restore health to you and heal your wounds, because they called you an outcast." (Jer 30:17)

"Restore to me the joy of your salvation." (Ps 51:12)

"Do not despise a thief who steals because he is hungry, but the thief who is caught must restore sevenfold." (Prv 6:30-31

" For your shame, you will have double and for confusion, they will rejoice in their portion. They will have everlasting joy." (Is 61:7)

~CHAPTER TWENTY-FOUR~

Back On Track

Wendy: Everything's Accelerated

Over the next couple of weeks, my acceleration took off with a series of events that were all to bring the miracle to pass. God began speaking to me about being ready for my husband. God started reminding me of people who were asked to do some very strange and even seemingly impossible things. Starting with: *Jonah* (prophet): Got scared, ran, screwed up. But God spat him out of the whale right back to where he was supposed to be.

Hosea (prophet): Asked to do a hard thing and marry a woman who would not be faithful, But God used him to reach others and to show the covenant between God and us.

Abigail (1 Sam 25) - Beautiful and Intelligent woman who God used to fix her husband's mistakes, right before they would be killed, But God made her brave and because she did not worry about her husband's wrath not only did God take care of her foolish husband he blessed her with the marriage to King David.

Esther - Rare, Beautiful, Adopted yet chosen by God to marry a king whose men wanted her and her people dead, But God made her brave and her obedience set God's people free.

Ruth - Forsaken, Widowed and without children, followed her Mother in law into a strange land But God gave her favor to marry a very wealthy man and restore a bloodline for Naomi.

All of these scriptures helped me to understand the way God thinks versus how I was thinking. I was eager to learn more from God about my new beginnings. It was amazing how much healing came from Eric admitting his part and me admitting mine. The healing happened instantly. Owning your stuff helps you transform from glory to glory. I had a great expectation that God would begin moving on Eric's behalf. I knew God would do the same for me, and whatever God would ask me to do I was ready to go full force back into ministry, but this time, I'll be waiting for God to lead. So grateful for all the healing. God is always faithful even when we screw up. Once we realigned ourselves with God's will, the acceleration was on and crackin'!

* *Eric called*: He repented for his absence and shared how he had preached his first sermon, in the midst of that discussion he stated how frustrated he was that something so great happened but he wasn't able to share it with me.

* *God revealed a huge aha moment for Eric:* This was, 'wow. He now saw why God never intended for him to do it (his career/ministry) alone.' This made me cry because he finally got how good God is and I was also remembering how painful and lonely ministry had been for me all those years. Eric got that revelation as well saying" Wow, how did you do it all those years?" I said, "God was too good to me not to."

* *Eric prays over me like a husband:* The very next day after Eric's revelation, I was hit by a car as I was crossing the parking lot. I called Eric to pray for. That was instinctively what I did without thinking. Hmmm. He was like, "Oh hell naw, this crap needs to stop now! "He prayed that He could be my covering and that this is the last time Satan gets to touch you. He also prayed God would accelerate me and bless me with the desires of my

heart.

God buys we a wedding dress: The following day, I went to meet with a lady about some vitamins, but instead, she told me God told her to give me $100. I looked at her confused, and she said yes, please take this and be blessed. I thanked God and then he told me to go the mall to a certain store he picked three dresses told me to try them on. I did with a puzzled look on my face. The third dress was long and flowy with crystals encrusted on the bust and waist. God said that's the one buy it. I was confused, huh this is like a wedding dress are you sure? God, it's expensive. He said do it. So, I got in line the lady said she was a Christian and she was to give me a discount. It came out to $100.00 even. God said use the money the lady gave you. As soon as I got to the car, I got a call from Eric asking how I was feeling? I told him what happened. He just started praising God. All night, God said, "You're mine, and you said I could give you to a man, correct?" I said, "Yes God, whatever you desire." He said, "My desires are to give you yours." I want you to be ready. I want you to go to Vegas, in three days.

*God gives me the funds to go to Vegas.

*God provides for Eric's trip to Vegas and makes a way out of none for His flight.

Eric: The Lion Awakens

The internet pastors I follow were exclaiming, "This is The Year of Jubilee," "double portion for your troubles," etc.. I was waiting to see. My new year wasn't starting off with a bang. Wendy had had a serious surgery during this time. Once she was back on her feet, she had a new zest for life. She had a pep in her step. She was back working with her son and getting back in tip-top shape. I told her I was so proud of her and her ability to overcome all obstacles.

One day she called me crying. I said, "What's wrong?" She said she had just been hit by a car. I'm like, "How do these things keep happening to you? She was shaken up, but fine, as she put it. I felt the protector rise up in my spirit and I started to pray differently, I prayed complete protection around her, and I commanded these attacks against her to stop, and that she would now be blessed, in Jesus name. By the time I finished praying, she was in brighter spirits and felt well enough to drive home. Something clicked that day within me. The words for prayers started flowing out of me with ease. It wasn't me; it was The Holy Spirit, but man, I got a glimpse of what a prayer warrior's prayer feels like.

The next day, Wendy called me to tell me something crazy just happened to her. I'm like, oh no, what now?. She said, "On the way to sign up with a lady for vitamins, she said, God told me to give you this 100.00 bill. Wendy was confused because she did not know this lady and she didn't owe her $100. But the lady insisted God told me to bless you.

After that, she continued on to the store and The Lord had her try on a couple of dresses. The Lord said get the 3rd one. She picked it and went to pay for it. The cashier gave her an employee discount just because (favor), and the total came to... $100. That dress ended up being her wedding dress.

We had been talking about the future in broad terms, looking at houses to rent, discussing our hearts desires for living and work, but not being personal.

During our conversations, The Lord would not allow me to talk about certain topics with her: sex, flirty stuff, marriage or say the big 3 words because last time I did it my way and look where it got us. God was doing a new thing.

So this time, we literally got to know each other all over again, and the distance kept us from ripping each other's clothes off. No internet camera stuff either. God was not playing this time. God let me see that Wendy always had my heart and knew me for me and still cared for me.

CALL TO ACTION:

If you had a chance to start over, how would you have done the courtship differently?

_____
_____
_____
_____
_____
_____

What rules would you have made for the relationship during your courtship and before your wedding?

_____
_____
_____
_____
_____

Would you have done your honeymoon differently if you knew what you knew now? If yes, how so?

_____
_____
_____

~CHAPTER TWENTY-FIVE~

The Leap Of Faith

Wendy: God Said Go

My sister in Vegas called that day you coming for Easter; I said I think I'm coming sooner if that's okay.. She said of course. Later that day I talked to Eric, I was fishing was it him? Had he talked to God about marrying me? He was very blunt if God told you to go then go. I said, but it's to get married. Who am I going to marry? He just said do you trust God I said yes he said then go. What the..!! I shared this with my roommate. She said, "God already told you who your husband was he doesn't change his mind! Trust him and go." So I said, "Okay God, I need money to go." God said, "Checks in the mail." So I packed my car. Went to the p.o. box. And sure enough, a check was in the mail. I took a picture and sent it to Eric. He said, "Okay, call me when you get there."

I got to Vegas and shared all these things about Eric with my sister, Melissa. She's spiritual, but she's never walked like me. So she just looked at me with a beautiful smile and said, Wendy if anyone deserves this you do, so just tell God I accept it. Tears flooded my face and I went to my room and finally asked, "God, am I marrying Eric?" He said, "Yes." Wow oh wow-oh God! I felt like I just hit a wall. It took me a minute to catch my breath. I just fell to my knees crying and praying in tongues.

I called Eric and told him that I was there. He says all matter-of-fact to me, "Okay, I'm finishing a script. I will buy my ticket tonight and be there Friday." Wait what!!! Oh God, this is for real-for real. My sister made massage and hair appointments. Eric emailed his itinerary and here we go. NOT! A huge windstorm came into Vegas. The sky was a foreboding black. Eric called. A huge storm hit Maryland, too. "Okay God was this all just a drill or is this really going down?" Eric, all calm and collect, says, "We trust God, right? He is just making everything sparkling for you."

"Okay," I said, he made me calm and reassured.

Then I got a text from my friend who set us up seven years ago Yes,Her, she asked "Are you and Eric getting married?", I said, 'It seems so."She said, "Well God told me, and I can't miss it, so I'm flying in Saturday." I said, "Okay, well I don't know anything, so that's up to you." Oh heck no! My nerves. Lord, I cannot take this. My sister said, 'It is ok; just calm down." I finally went to sleep. I awoke to Eric's text saying his flight was canceled as well as all remaining flights. "Okay God, I know this is all you, so I will just keep my peace." I tried calling Eric and couldn't get a hold of him. "Okay God, me and you. What's happening?" God just said, "Trust me." I went back to sleep. The next day I got an email from Eric with his new flight info. "Okay, here we go."

I got up, got dressed (twice). Then it hit me, "Oh God, I have not seen this man in 6.5 years!!" I picked him up from the airport. From the first moment I laid eyes on him, I knew God was faithful and this man is my husband. A flood of emotions came over me, yet everything just flowed like no time had ever passed. He grabbed me close hugged me right and laid an amazing kiss on me that wow was even more passionate than before. I looked in his eyes, and I could see the spark had never left. That's truly the grace of God. We went and saw his daughter and spent the whole day just laughing and having fun. Remember I had not seen Eric in 6.5 years. BUT God...

After the party, we went to get a smoothie and Eric poured his heart out to me. He shared everything that up till now God had told him he couldn't. He told me how much he loves me, how he cannot wait to be my husband, how much he's looking forward to ministry together and so much more! I felt every word and every emotion he was feeling and then I knew this is God's timing, not ours. We cried, we laughed, and we were just, real 100 percent real, with each other and ourselves. After we held each other for a long time. We left and went to the courthouse got the license and as we were leaving a young guy came to our car and asked us if we were looking to have a Christian ceremony. What. We just looked at each other laughed and said, 'it's all, you God!" We were in control of nothing but to be obedient! He literally made a way where there was no way!!!! He was into all the details. God was for us and nothing, and nobody could be against us. But God knows your heart better than you.

Eric: What Happened In Vegas

After finishing up a writing job, some money came in for me. I wanted to surprise my daughter, now living in Vegas, for her 9th birthday. Her birthday party was set for April 1. I bought my plane ticket for the 31st. On the 31st, all flights going to Vegas were canceled from DC because of a thunderstorm in DC and a sandstorm in Vegas. No, you don't, devil! God got this. Wendy was upset. She thought God lied to her again. She talked to me, and I was like, "We are in God's hands now. No need to stress out. What's one day?" I flew in the next day. She picked me up from the airport, and it was like no time had passed. She was as beautiful as ever. Sexy, electrifying smile. Lustrous hair. We hugged for an eternity; then I planted a soft kiss on her soft lips. "Ahhh Ahhh Ahhh Ahhh Ahhh," the angels sang. Yep, we still got it. We hopped in her truck and drove to my daughter's birthday party holding hands the whole time.

The party was amazing. My daughter was so surprised. We had a great time. Her mom and I got along just fine. Her and Wendy talked and laughed while I played games with my daughter and her friends. This is what I missed all of those years. Just being with my daughter. Ooh, I felt on top of the world.

We pulled over to get smoothies, and now for the first time in years, God let me share my whole heart and emotions with Wendy. I allowed myself to be vulnerable and finally told Wendy how much I loved her and missed her. How she was a rock for me. How much I thought about her over the years. We hugged and kissed ever so warmly. Then we looked into each other eyes and said at the same time, "we need to go get our license." We headed to downtown Vegas and paid for our license.

A young man approached us and asked if we were looking for a chapel with a Christian Pastor? We said yes, and he took us to meet her. After talking with her for a few minutes, she asked what we do? We said we were ministers. She said, "I thought so." She then told me if I didn't have a tux, she could rent me one for... wait for it... for free, it's normally 100.00. Wendy and I did a double take and laughed. Then she proceeded to tell us the packages, but for you, I will give the deluxe for 100.00. We could not believe all this favor.

I had to buy the ring in Vegas because literally God said go and I hopped on a plane. So I went looking for the ring and found it at a local jeweler. I went in, and as I was looking over the various rings, God said, "That one! Like a true man, I looked at the price tag first. "I got this," but then I saw another one. I was like, 'How about this? God said, "I already told you which one." So I got the God one.

CALL TO ACTION:

How has God shown you favor in your past or present relationships?

_____

_____

_____

_____

_____

~CHAPTER TWENTY-SIX~

Wedding The Bells!

Wendy: *Fo Real Fo Real*

The day of our wedding was amazing. I in my dress and he in a suit stood in this little chapel hand-picked by God. My sister on my side and our friend on his. Eric and I were ready; we knew that it was time to do this. As we shared gazes, smiles, vows and much more. God reassured us with his amazing presence. We anointed each other with oil (the oil God had had me make all those years before) and took our first communion as husband and wife. As soon as we said Amen, the holy spirit came upon us and we laughed and broke out in tongues.

> *"And there came a voice from heaven, saying, Thou art my beloved Son, in whom I am well pleased." Mk 1:11*

Our love was so strong for each other; even the Pastor began to cry. My sister shed tears and said it was so beautiful and you both have so much love for each other. I looked Eric in the eyes with so much love, longing, joy and now hope for our new lives. "my husband "I whispered. "My wife," he said, and pulled me into him, and we kissed. But God. He is so faithful.

Eric: Married & Blessed

The wedding was in a quaint chapel and officiated by a Christian pastor. We prayed, took communion and anointed each other during our ceremony. It was beautiful. Wendy looked stunning in her white dress. As it was happening, I couldn't believe it was happening. God did this. God brought us back together. God brought me a stunning, radiant bride. God, you're so so good!

{Note: After the wedding, Wendy told me this was the ring that she told God she wanted. It's such a blessing to know that God, Wendy and I are on the same page. What a way to start a marriage!}

Afterwards, I had to get back to MD with my mom. I stayed with her for another month until the Lord said, "That's it. Get back to LA and your wife." I was on a plane back to LA the next morning. It was hell getting back to LA, but since I've been back, Wendy and I haven't been apart a single day. I know you're saying, duh, you're married now, but the Lord has stuffed so much into the three months following our wedding, we haven't had time to breathe. We've moved from hotel to hotel for an entire 6 weeks. We are experts on hotels now. We have been by each other's side day and night. God is doing a new thing through us, and we are blessed and privileged that He would choose us to walk this journey together. A journey that looked doomed 7 years ago. Now, we are married, doing ministry, writing books, being each other's best friend, loving each other, laughing with each other, and learning each other all over again... Now that ain't nothing *But Gaawwdd!*

~CHAPTER TWENTY-SEVEN~

Sex Is Great For The Soul

The Holy Spirit to Eric & Wendy: Let Love Rein

Sex between a husband and his wife is the truest expression of complete intimacy through Christ Jesus. The completed work. Normally when you think of sex, especially when you're single, you're not thinking of God being a part of it. Christians have trained themselves to either abstain (not date) or be celibate (date without sex) in order to train our flesh to submit to the spirit. And it is not so much that you are abstaining from pleasure or suppressing your flesh, but rather you are presevering yourself and your oil (your gifts intended for your spouse).

Jesus wants you to keep from giving up your oil. By keeping yourself and your body set apart from the lusts of the world, you stay strong and keep your reserves stored up for when you are married. This alone is reason enough to not fornicate (sex before marriage), masturbate (self-gratify), or commit adultery(sex, lust or intimacy with someone other than your spouse), because this belongs to your mate. Imagine both you and your future spouse doing the same. You both are storing up treasures (gifts, blessings, oil, healing, inheritance) in heaven that will be released only to each other.
Take a few minutes and meditate on this. Let that sink in... ... ...

When you are single, you are heirs of God and joint-heirs with Christ. Christ is alive in you. You have become his holy temple. The marriage between you and God is complete and whole to, a degree. God will not tempt you. He will deliver you from temptation if you truly submit yourself to him and come into agreement that you will remain celibate for Him, yourself, and your future mate. Hence, in Song of Solomon 8:4 it warns us "to not stir up love before its time." And in Matthew 5:28, it warns you "to not even look lustfully at another woman/man." That is because your Father in heaven wants you to save all of that for your mate so that when you marry, your soul mate you become one flesh, a completed work, "a three stranded cord" (Eccl. 4:12). "Where two or more gathered, there he is in the midst" (Matt.18:20).

This is why God warns his children (you) not to fornicate or masturbate because the act itself bonds you to the very person you are having sex with. It also creates a cord that can not be easily broken, called a soul tie (see Prayer to Break Soul Ties in Appendix B to break soul ties. FYI, you can pray and ask God to break the soul tie, but its His choice whether or not he does or doesn't). You're knowingly or unknowingly attaching this person to your destiny that may not be a part of it. You're choosing one night stands, quickies, and booty calls over the soul mate God's been preparing for you, your purpose, and your destiny. Is it really worth that? Hell naw! 1 Cor 6: 15-20 says it all:

> "Do you not know that your bodies are members of Christ himself? Shall I then take the members of Christ and unite them with a prostitute? Never! Do you not know that he who unites himself with a prostitute is one with her in body? For it is said, "The two will become one flesh." But whoever is united with the Lord is one with him in spirit. Flee from sexual immorality. All other sins a person commits are outside the body, but whoever sins sexually, sins against their own body. Do you not know that your bodies are temples of the Holy Spirit, who is in you, whom you have received from God? You are not your own; you were bought at a price. Therefore honor God with your bodies."

Now on to our married couples...

"The marriage bed is undefiled because his perfect will is in it" Heb.13:4

When you got married and joined in covenant with God, Jesus, and The Holy Spirit, you both now have the ability to go to the third heaven to be a ministry unto one another. You can receive impartations, gifts and strength from God together! This is huge in developing trust, tenderness and mercies. This is why the enemy would rather you partake of counterfeit intimacy: watch porn, masturbate or satisfy lust-filled urges of adultery. He doesn't want you to receive the true, intense intimacy of God that allows you to become one ,bonded and rooted in HIM. Satan is all about the counterfeit love: orgies, porn, swinging, speed-dating, reality dating TV shows, Romance novels and strip clubs. The menage-e-trios is a perversion of the three-stranded cord relationship between husband-wife-God. Satan will do anything he can to pervert this perfect form of ministry.

So many people think one of the two ways about sex in marriage: before salvation, it's a release to an urge it's a way of self-gratifying or in marriage and usually after salvation, you now feel obligated to be with each other because your bodies no longer belong to yourselves, but to each other. Both are a fraction of its true meaning. Marriage is the highest form of ministry there is.

Husbands, you should see yourself humbly as a king being given a crown of glory (the woman) (Prv 12:4) What an incredible honor God is bestowing upon you when you find a wife.

So let's break this down. First, God created man and then said he needed a helpmate, so he pulled her out of him. Let that sink in for a minute. That does not mean she is less than him, it means she is a part of him. In Webster's dictionary it says the function of the rib is to help in protecting and supporting the vital organs such as the heart and lungs (protection; under-girding), allows the breathing to occur (peace). It's the wife that creates this barrier to a man's heart. She is his protection for the heart and breath. She is a gift, a treasure. To go even deeper, she helps with the flow of the blood (Christ) and the breath of life (the Holy Spirit).

Second, God says "be fruitful and multiply." You can not do this alone. It takes two, in the natural order of things, to create another gift (child) from God. Just as God asks you not to rob him of his tithes and offerings (Mal 3:8), He does not want you to hoard the love, intimacy and sexual healing that was put in you to give to your partner. This to him is an offering. His offering.

1 Corinthians 7:3-5 reads:

> *"Let the husband render to his wife the affection due her, and likewise also the wife to her husband. The wife does not have authority over her own body, but the husband does. And likewise*

the husband does not have authority over his own body, but the wife does. Do not deprive one another except with consent for a time, that you may give yourselves to fasting and prayer; and come together again so that Satan does not tempt you.

God did not give you permission to withhold His gifts: sex, affection, blessings, healing, love, intimacy, encouragement and support meant for your spouse, from your spouse. You are stealing God's offerings to your spouse that he entrusted to you. That is called being a thief, an embezzler, a hoarder. What is commandment #3? "Thou shalt not steal."

Third, He says you're now in a covenant with Christ, joint heirs in him so you need to be equally yoked (2 Cor 6:14). See God, our God, created a way after the fall of man to preserve the covenant with him. You and your partner need to have one common goal, dream and destiny or you will split that baby (marriage) in half and it will die.

Fourth, the level of intimacy through sex between a husband and wife is inclusive of God being present to bring forth life. As your Creator, this is His pleasure, His honor to meet you two in this holy place (the undefiled bed) and bring forth the birth of life, creation and ministry. It allows you two who have been apart to now come together as one and truly become one flesh.

Imagine if you had this revelation when you were single and a virgin. Imagine if you had collected your own tears and put them in a bottle for your wedding day. Imagine if as you prayed and ushered in the Lord, that oil came forth that you collected for your wedding day. Wow the power of this. In Song of Solomon 5: 2-6, He gives us a picture of this:

> "I was asleep but my heart was awake.
> A voice! My beloved was knocking
> Open to me, my sister, my darling
> My dove my perfect one
> For my head is drenched with dew my locks with the damp of the night...
> (God desire's to minister to you two. He stands there morning till night)
> ... I have taken off my dress--How can I put it on again?
> I have washed my feet how can I dirty them again?
> My beloved extended his hand through the opening and my feelings were aroused for him...
> (You have asked for God to heal, yet when he comes you deny him)
> ... I arose to open to my beloved and my hands were dripped with myrrh, and my fingers with liquid myrrh, On the handles of the bolt...
> (He had come to bring you healing, restoration, a blessing, yet you rejected it because it was not the vessel or the way you wanted it to come, however the very key to your blessings resides in your mate)
> ... I opened to my beloved. But my beloved had turned away and had gone. My heart went out to him as he spoke. I searched for him, I called him but he did not answer me."
> (Yes you not only rejected your mate you rejected the one who brought him/her to you, you grieved The Holy Spirit)

Let's break this scripture down a little more. See, we know God hears our cries. He knows our hearts; and He is always talking to us. But if we have a preconceived idea of what that should look like, you could miss an opportunity to receive from Him. Your spouse is just that, a love offering a gift from God. It is God who stirs him/her up and arouses him/her so that you will be drawn into one another. And who will be right in the middle of you two? God, himself, will be right there in the midst. Glory!

In verse 5, He says, "I arose to open to my beloved and my hands were dripped with myrrh, and my fingers with liquid myrrh, on the handles of the bolt (door knob). On the door knob means you were given keys to healing, protection and prosperity by coming to one another at his calling.

Let's talk about liquid myrrh for a second. Myrrh is mentioned in the Bible 152 times. Myrrh was used to enhance, as a natural healing remedy, and to purify the dead. Enhance, heal, purify, remember that. Now let's go deeper. What are the benefits of liquid myrrh? Myrrh oil is one of the gifts, along with gold and frankincense, that the three wise men brought to Jesus as gifts from the king.

Myrrh is the sap of the tree called Commiphora, grown in the deserts of Africa and the Middle East. Its trunk is usually twisted from the harsh weather-- hmm, like Jesus the tree of life, twisted and beaten for us--with few leaves and a white flower. However, to get to the myrrh, the trunk must be cut into to release the resin. The resin is allowed to dry and begins to look like tears all along the trees trunk. The resin is then collected and used to create oil from the sap.

So why would God use this allegory to speak to us about the love between the husband and wife? Why was this a gift to Jesus? So many things come to me as I write this. The greatest is that a painstaking procedure must occur in order to release this resin. This gift and its powerful properties bring healing in a way that preserves your life, fights disease and binds you two together for His purpose and for His glory.

So how could this unconditional love offering, the gift of intimacy, be tainted? By overstimulating our eye gates with pornography, promiscuous sex, sexual imagery, and the 'sex sells' mantra in advertisements through the media. It promotes lust, but that is something you have power and control of, right? But what if it is greater than this. What if this 'offering' is God showing up in the midst of your marriage and struggle to bring you a level of healing that can literally preserve your life, cancel every attack, and restore you to a place of greater love, revelation, and intimacy than you could have ever imagined before? What if it's a gift to reward you for withstanding the harsh storms of life and bring forth a resin that can grow your home, your ministry and literally prepare you for the work, the greater work in God?! Hallelujah! What if that person lying next to you could release a level of healing through their touch that would release the Glory and splendor of your king and transport you both to heavenly places where only the truest of love resides in him?

Are you beginning to see and feel how glorious a marriage can be with God as your center?

If this is how God sees the marriage, the marriage bed, and sex (intimacy), then the key to sex is literally the banquet. Huh? What? The banquet? What banquet? The banquet in Psalms 23. The banquet "in front of your enemy." Remember?

> "You prepare a table before me in the presence of my enemies. You anoint my head with oil; my cup overflows."

Who is David talking to when he says, "You prepare a table...?" God! God prepares a table for you in the presence of your enemies. Why would God do that? Because it is the enemy who's doing everything possible to rob, steal, kill and destroy your marriage. But God delivers you out of every possible attack the enemy tries to attack you with. Every weapon that the enemy throws at your marriage, God's got the defense to it. The enemy throws sickness at you. God heals you (Jer 33:6). The enemy throws strife and division; God comes back with peace (Jn 16:33) and intimacy (Gen 2:18). The banquet table is where healing, love, grace, mercy and trust can grow and overflow into every area of your being. Its the covenant. The place of consecration. His marriage to you both creates the beautiful aroma of love in a new wine skin with the purest and finest of wine flowing to overflowing, all in the presence of your enemies.

What about the table? Is it just a normal table with some turkey and cranberry sauce on it? No, it's God's table. What does God's table look like? Let's find out. In Exodus 25, The Lord tells Moses to tell the Israelites to make a tabernacle for Him. He goes on to tell Moses what to put in it: The Ark chest and atonement cover, The Table, The Lampstand, etc.. We'll focus on The Table of The Lord in verses 23-30:

The Table

"Make a table of acacia wood—two cubits long, a cubit wide and a cubit and a half high. Overlay it with pure gold and make a gold molding around it. Also make around it a rim a handbreadth wide and put a gold molding on the rim. Make four gold rings for the table and fasten them to the four corners, where the four legs are. The rings are to be close to the rim to hold the poles used in carrying the table. Make the poles of acacia wood, overlay them with gold and carry the table with them. And make its plates and

dishes of pure gold, as well as its pitchers and bowls for the pouring out of offerings. Put the bread of the Presence on this table to be before me at all times."

This is the table God set for you and your marriage. God set a table for You! Partake of it with you and your spouse and He will anoint your head with 'oil'. Your marriage cup shall overflow (with love, healing, prosperity, protection, intimacy, fruitfulness). Surely His goodness and love will follow your marriage all the days of your lives, and you both will dwell in the house of the Lord forever.

(Meditate (Selah) on what God is saying to you in this scripture about your marriage...)

Are you beginning to realize how important marriage is to God? Good. Now let's breakdown Ps 23 line by line to see what else God is saying to you:

1 The Lord is my shepherd; I shall not want. (You have no wants)

2 He makes me to lie down in green pastures; (Rest)

He leads me beside the still waters. (He brings you living water aka Jesus; Peace)

3 He restores my soul; (Restoration, Healing, Empowerment)

He guides me in the paths of righteousness For His name's sake. (He leads me down the same paths (victories, healings, power, blessings and ministry that he led Jesus)

4 Yea, though I walk through the valley of the shadow of death, I

will fear no evil; For You are with me (Even though you will go through tough times and walk among the dead,(unbelievers) you have nothing to fear because He is with you

Your rod and Your staff, they comfort me. (He has given you power, authority and dominion as he says in regards to the rod (authority) staff (shepherd). They are to comfort you until you come again into the bed chambers as you are urged and stirred with arousal for your mate after this weary travel)

5 You prepare a table before me in the presence of my enemies; You anoint my head with oil; My cup runs over. (Together you two create the banquet where true love can now reside and nurture and feed your very souls,

6 Surely goodness and mercy shall follow me. All the days of my life (This is a promise from God that you will have goodness and mercy all the days of your life)

And I will dwell in the house of the Lord (This brings forth God's holy myrrh and keeps you in the house of the Lord

Forever."

(Eternity)

Tell me that isn't a joyous covenant to be a part of! If you're married, you already are! (Eric's doing his Michael Jackson dance as I'm writing this...lol) We bet, with a few tweaks, your marriage can thrive the way God intended it to.

Are you withholding God's gifts for your spouse?

Are you robbing God and your spouse of the things rightfully due them within your marriage?

Are you embezzling or hoarding affection due your spouse/marriage and ultimately yourself?

FYI, I asked the same question three different ways to make a point. If you answered 'yes' to any of these questions, you are selling yourself, your spouse, and God short. But being the merciful God that He is, He has put a remedy right in the Bible. One scripture in particular brings forth the love, jubilee, and pure joy every marriage should have. Proverbs 17:22 reads: "A merry heart does good like medicine But a broken spirit dries the bones."

Merry means:

1. Showing high spirits or lightheartedness
2. Cheerful
3. Joyous
4. Uninhibited enjoyment of frolic or festivity
5. Carefree
6. Innocent
7. Heedless gaiety
8. Elation and exhilaration of spirits

9. Singing, dancing

10. Good fellowship

11. High spirits expressed in laughing, bantering, jesting

Now let's look at 'Broken':

1. Violently separated into parts

2. Damaged or altered

3. Not working properly

4. Being irregular, interrupted, or full of obstacles

5. Violated by transgression :not kept or honored, a broken promise

6. Discontinuous

7. Disrupted by change

8. Having an irregular, streaked, or blotched pattern especially from virus infection

9. Made weak or infirm

10. Subdued completely :crushed, sorrowful

11. Bankrupt

12. Reduced in rank

13. Cut off, disconnected, speak a few broken words

14. Not complete or full

15. Disunited by divorce, separation, or desertion

Which list of words does your marriage most identify with right this moment?

If you're answered the 'broken' list, I say to you right now, you can change it. You can reverse course. But you must start with repentenance for being selfish or self-centered, (whether knowingly or unknowingly) hand your relationship back to God, submitting and realigning your will to His, forgiving all of your spouses wrongs, and make a concerted effort everyday not to hoard or embezzle the affection, love, healing, oil, and blessings due him/her.. While you do that, speak God's Word over the dry bones of your relationship just like Ezekiel did (Ez 37:4-7:

"Again He said to me, "Prophesy to these bones, and say to them, 'O dry bones, hear the word of the Lord! Thus says the Lord God to these bones: "Surely I will cause breath to enter into you, and you shall live. I will put sinews on you and bring flesh upon you, cover you with skin and put breath in you; and you shall live. Then you shall know that I am the Lord.""" So I prophesied as I was commanded; and as I prophesied, there was a noise, and suddenly a rattling; and the bones came together, bone to bone..."

Prophesy to your dry marriage o' son/daughter of Man. Call forth all of God's promises and blessings that he has bestowed on those who are in covenant with Him in the Name of Jesus! In financial troubles, command Prosperity to come! Loveless marriage, command Love come! In a bitter relationship, command forgiveness and Laughter to return in Jesus name! In a non-affectionate, sexless marriage, command Sex to reignite! Command all of God's blessings with your names on it to come to you now from the north, south, east and west in the name of Jesus! Speak sons/daughters of Man! Speak!

God's perfect design was for Adam and Eve to live with Him in paradise. He withheld no good thing from them. There was no lack. The curse of lack came in after they gave into the lie that they were somehow missing something. No, they were God's completed work! You and your spouse are God's completed work! They had everything. God's gifts produce life and overflow more exceedingly and abundantly than all you can ask or think. So embrace one another. See yourself and your spouse as true gifts from God to each other. Treat one another with tenderness and goodness. Allow the Holy Spirit to nudge you into each other's arms. See it as God waking you both from a peaceful night's rest of spooning and gently whispering to you all, "Come on you two; there's a celebration at the banquet table right now in your honor. Come and join me."

~EPILOGUE~

Eric & Wendy: Final Words

In the weeks after the marriage, Eric would anoint my feet daily or read the word over me as we went to sleep. We'd be in the car and he would be singing and worshiping right with me. Any time either of us heard from God, the other would finish the thought or the word God gave us. It was crazy how natural all this spiritual stuff came to us considering we had been apart all these years.

The first revelation God gave me was that for 23 years that I was married to my first husband I was faithful to do all God told me to do for him including forgiveness. God said those seeds were sown faithfully and so in this new marriage to Eric you are reaping ALL those seeds. Because they were sown out of obedience, God will reward those efforts, not necessarily the person you are doing the acts to, But God. Wow God is so faithful.

The second revelation God gave me is that when Eric had oiled my feet and gave me my first foot massage on our very first date, that in actuality, God had him anoint me and bless me without him even having the revelation, but simply out of obedience., I am reminded of how Ruth was told by Naomi to lay the blanket across Boaz's feet in the Book of Ruth 3:24-28:

> "So she lay at his feet until morning, but got up before anyone could be recognized; and he said, "No one must know that a woman came to the threshing floor." (He protected her honor) He also said, "Bring me the shawl you are wearing and hold it out." When she did so, he poured into it six measures of barley and placed the bundle on her. Then he went back to town. (Boaz was a blessing to her and her family, not a taker) When Ruth came to her mother-in-law, Naomi asked, "How did it go, my daughter?" Then she told her everything Boaz had done for her and added, "He gave me these six measures of barley, saying, 'Don't go back to your mother-in-law empty-handed. Then Naomi said, "Wait, my daughter, until you find out what happens. For the man will not rest until the matter is settled today." (God is letting us women know that if we are still, God will stir the Man up and the man will do whatever he's told so that he can have God's promise, which includes a wife.)

Waiting is actually very good for you. God promises if you wait (rest in HIM) that your heart will be strengthened.

> "Wait on the Lord Be of good courage, And He shall strengthen your heart, Wait, I say, on the Lord!..." Ps 27:14 (NKJV)
> Stay focused on God's promises and not a man's empty words.

Trust me when God tells him to move he will move, and nothing will stop him. You really can trust God in all things. See for the longest time I was focused on what I was seeing the other person do or not do. I was using the scripture, "free will" in the wrong context which brought fear into me. If I really had understood this principle then doubt and mostly fear would not have come over me the day Eric said, "Go do you," because the truth was God knew Eric's heart and knew he wanted this life. He knew Eric was just struggling with letting go of his old self, his old identity. It was never about, 'another woman,' it was Eric making sure he would not regret letting go of his past or his dreams. Eric has soon learned after we got married that he didn't let go of anything in regards to his dreams, he accelerated them by attaching them to his destiny, and by marrying me, his gift and a partner who is in agreement.

To God be the glory for he is a miraculous God and he is always on time. Now we have to walk this new road together. God has been strategically showing us who to have in our sphere and how to do this new life as one. As you well know, we both had been through so much, so with that healing and/or warfare does come. Iron is definitely sharpening iron right now. Three key things God gave me were this:

1) Be transparent with each other. Well, this was a basic rule Eric

had already established when we were just friends and it helped tremendously. However, now that we are married and living under the same roof it is even more of necessity.

2) Have fun. Learn from one another. Spending quality time together. Making sure life becomes balanced is super key right now. You can become very serious when you are trying to protect what God has given you. Give yourself permission to breathe and to even make mistakes. You two are adjusting. Live by 1 Cor 13: 4-13:

> "Love is patient; love is kind. It does not envy, it does not boast, it is not proud. It does not dishonor others; it is not self-seeking, it is not easily angered, it keeps no record of wrongs. Love does not delight in evil but rejoices with the truth. It always protects, always trusts, always hopes, always perseveres. Love never fails. But where there are prophecies, they will cease; where there are tongues, they will be stilled; where there is knowledge, it will pass away. For we know in part and we prophesy in part, but when completeness comes, what is in part disappears. When I was a child, I talked like a child, I thought like a child, I reasoned like a child. When I became a man, I put the ways of childhood behind me. For now, we see only a reflection as in a mirror; then we shall see face to face. Now I know in part; then I shall know fully, even as I am fully known. And now these three remain: faith, hope and love. But the greatest of these is love."

And thirdly, grace and mercy at all times. Talking isn't enough. You also need to discuss the why. The why may not even be you, but you're learning how your spouse thinks and feels. So give each other room to do so without getting offended. Both of us had to work hard on this we were not only defensive but shut down for so long in some areas that we were just real raw. Again that's ok; God's got you. Hearing is the second part of this. You must be able to listen to your mate. Listen with an open heart and mind, not wanting to fix them or change them, but to embrace and truly accept each other.

Pain and triggers are real, just don't claim them. Instead, figure out the root of it. Pull that root out and replace it with God's love and scripture. Watch how quickly healing, trust and respect comes. Eric was key in helping me build new boundaries with both friends and family. He was able to help me prioritize myself, so my healing would stick. I was key in lifting Eric up and letting him be the head of the household and taking our prayer life to a new level so he could hear God clearly. My job is helpmate, not nag and it's God's job to show Eric, and it's Eric's job to obey. We have always loved to read and worshiped together.. Eric also honored God and went off social media for 6 months. He repented to my son and to Pastor Mel, his family, and many others. He truly has been walking out his healing, and this has helped build my trust in the God in him

The Call To Salvation Prayer

If anyone reading this book has not given their life to Jesus Christ and want to know that you're going to heaven , please read the prayer below and join us in the Kingdom of God.

Lord God,

I want you in my life. I need to know you. I need a relationship with you. Be my Lord. Be my savior. Forgive me for all of my sins. Thank you for sending your only begotten son, Jesus Christ, to die on the cross for me and resurrecting him. From this day forward, Jesus Christ is the Lord of my life. Forever and ever. Amen

If you said this prayer, congratulations!, you are now a Child of God. Your life will never be the same. Please write to us and let us know you have given your life to Christ. Welcome brother and sister in Christ!

Make sure you sign up for Eric & Wendy's Facebook page @ EW Ingram to keep updated on their free giveaways, newest books, devotionals, in-store book signings, speaking engagements, seminars, boot camps and movies.

<u>Coming attractions:</u>

The Prodigal Couple Mens & Womens Devotional
The Prodigal Couple Prayer Book
The Prodigal Couple YouTube Channel

What Now?

* Join our social media family :   Facebook - EW Ingram

   Twitter - @prodigalcouple

   Instagram - #theprodigalcouple

* Sign up for the prodigal couple website to keep updated with coming attractions, blogs, events, and merchandise at www.prodigalcouple.com

* Reread the book with your spouse/partner. Answer any question that you could not during your initial reading.

* Meditate on the scriptures pertaining to your issues in this book. What is the Holy Spirit telling you to do about them?

* Dig deeper into the notes you made. Ask The Holy Spirit to reveal what vows you made that became the root of your negative behavior. Once the issues are revealed, immediately pray this:

Lord, thank you for revealing (issue/problem/lie of the enemy/vow). I ask that you pull up the root out of my heart and replace it with (find scriptures that say what God says about that issue), I.e., if bitterness is your issue, you would say, I ask that you pull that root out of my heart and replace it with Hebrews 12:15: "See to it that no one fails to obtain the grace of God; that no "root of bitterness" springs up and causes trouble, and by it many become defiled." In Jesus' Mighty Name, Amen.

* If any topic/subject in this book offended you, ask The Holy Spirit why it offended you? That may be the revealing of a root you need to pull up and get rid of so you can be healed in that area of your life.

* Have the talk about the issues that led the relationship astray

* Pray together in the morning, noon, and night about healing your relationship

* Start a study group with other couples

* Do some spring cleaning! Get rid of old memorabilia from your old self and start fresh and new. Create new, God-filled memories!

* Journal all of the new blessings that the Lord is bestowing on you and your relationship.

* Before you go to work and before you go to bed, give your spouse 5 biblical compliments that God says about them. (You can add a couple, but start with the Biblical ones to start building up their spirit man/woman)

~APPENDIX A~

Eric & Wendy's 8-Year Timeline

"We let counterfeit love, hurt, distractions and egos get in the way of God's perfect love affair."

Wendy	Eric
Got divorced, overcame sickness	Had a baby
Received word from God about new husband	Received a prophecy of things to come
Met Eric (the one)	Met Wendy (the one)
God confirmed prophecy	Prophecy revealed; Wendy & mantle
Separated from Eric	Separated from Wendy
Got mad at God, wanted control	Still wanted "old life," be in control
Fell hard, was miserable	Made choices w/o God/was miserable
Kept longing for Eric	Kept wanting Wendy
Started seeking God again	Desperately needed to hear God again
Health & Abusive relationship caused her to run back to God	Father's sudden passing caused him to surrender all to God
Heard from Eric. Let go of victim self and asked Eric for forgiveness	Contacted Wendy. Let go of old self and asked Wendy for forgiveness
God's Grace flooded our lives	
Rcvd God's gift and love through Eric	Rcvd God's gift and love through Wendy
Started following God's voice daily	Finally accepted mantle
Left abusive relationship & health and began being restored	Became a minister
Drove to Vegas on Faith	Flew to Vegas on Faith
Got Married!	
"Therefore a man shall leave his father and mother and be joined to his wife, and they shall become one flesh." Gen 2:24	

Eric & Wendy's Marriage Bootcamp

* Engagement/Preparation For Marriage:

These tips will set the tone for a successful marriage.

-- Believe God for your spouse.

-- Stay celibate.

-- Take authority over your flesh.

-- Cut off social media.

-- No masturbation

-- Eat right (no drugs or alcohol)

-- Exercise Together. Start teaching your body to submit to you, not you submitting to your urges or thoughts. You are not alone. We all have them. But when you start training your body to submit to you and the Word of God, then God can trust you to train others. Control your body and urges it is a sign of Christ maturing in you.

-- Testing is of God. He knows our flesh, but if we call on the name of Jesus, we have the power to rule over our flesh. Temptation is not from God.

-- Be the Master of your heart and thoughts. This is training for later when your spouse comes. You need to have this in place. It's harder after you meet him/her.

* Anchor Your Foundation In The Word

Eph 5: 22-33 is our marital foundation:

> "Wives, submit to your own husbands, as to the Lord. For the husband is head of the wife, as also Christ is head of the church; and He is the Savior of the body. Therefore, just as the church is subject to Christ, so let the wives be to their own husbands in everything. Husbands, love your wives, just as Christ also loved the church and gave Himself for her, that He might sanctify and cleanse her with the washing of water by the word, that He might present her to Himself a glorious church, not having spot or wrinkle or any such thing, but that she should be holy and without blemish. So husbands ought to love their own wives as their own bodies; he who loves his wife loves himself. For no one ever hated his own flesh, but nourishes and cherishes it, just as the Lord does the church. For we are members of His body, of His flesh and His bones. "For this reason, a man shall leave his father and mother and be joined to his wife, and the two shall become one flesh. This is a great mystery, but I speak concerning Christ and the church. Nevertheless, let each one of you in particular so love his own wife as himself, and let the wife see that she respects her husband..."

Gal 5: 16-21 - What Not To Allow In Your Marriage

Gal 5 22-26 - What To Do In Your Marriage

1 Cor 13: 4-9 - How to Love Your Spouse

1 Corinthians 7: 1-16 - How To Treat Your Spouse/Do Ministry

With Your Partner

Obey God's Word <u>and</u> his chosen leaders.

* Newlywed/Separated/On The Verge Of Divorce:

Here are some of the things we established right off the bat:

-- God is head of our household and our lives: (Joshua 24:15)

-- Lay your whole life down at Jesus feet. (*Mt 10:39*)

-- Ask Jesus to be your lord and savior

-- Pick up your cross(calling) and follow Him. (*Lk 9:23*)

-- Dedicate your firsts to Him. (*Deut 26*)

-- Your time. 2.40 hours of every 24 minimum. (*Lev. 27:30*) In prayer, worship, thanksgiving, and reading your word.

-- We made each other our first ministry (Deut 24:5)

-- *Create a prayer life together morning and night* (this is different than just praying together, it's establishing what you are praying for) (*Joshua 1:8*)

-- *Speak Life* (The Word) not death over each other

-- Claim His promises for you and your family daily

-- Do Not Pray Your Own Will, Pray For God's WIll For Your Life

-- Follow His commandments

-- *Trust God to right your wrongs* -- Don't fight battles you don't need to. Forgive everyone you don't need to. Forgive everyone who has ever offended you. No matter how hard it is, you're letting go of something that has drained you of your strength and purpose. --

-- Let Go & Let God as they say. Show them the grace God's given you for your mistakes.

-- *Don't fight or argue with people.* Do your warfare in prayer.

-- Keep your peace. Self-control.(2Tim 1:7)

-- *Let go of your old self.* Let God change your heart, mind, vision, and purpose for your life.

-- Create a budget and a schedule (to include time for each other (Rom 13:8)

-- *Tithes & Offerings*: Give your first 10% to your local church and ask God where He wants you to give your love offering. (*Mal 3:10*)

-- *Find a Bible-based church* where you will be members and *serve!* Don't just go to get fed but be ready to help.

Accountability – Find an honorable Christian couple and let them mentor you.

Tithing - Not just money, it's also time, talents, resources

Get planted in your local church together: Volunteer, serve, greet, Do something! Serving God is serving the church, not man

-- *Gather your "12" partners/disciples* for ministry and business (*Mk 1*)

-- *Discuss what type of marriage you desire*, and then make a plan on how you can take daily, weekly and yearly goals to nurture it. (*Hab 2: 2-3*)

-- *Set your argument/disagreement rules:* Give your spouse the benefit of the doubt. Take a deep breath before responding in a critical fashion. (*1 Cor 13*)

"... Everyone should be quick to listen, slow to speak and slow to anger..." (James 1:19)

-- *Set healthy boundaries for friends and family.* The marriage is between you, your spouse and God. Any other input is just merely suggestions and opinions. (*Gen 2: 24*)

-- Take the first year to build the foundation of your marriage.

> *"If a man has recently married, he must not be sent to war or have any other duty laid on him. For one year he is to be free to stay at home and bring happiness to the wife he has married."*
> *(Deut 24:5)*

-- Don't make choices without consulting God. He's your Partner. (Mt 6:33)

-- *Start telling others about Christ.* Share how he has changed your life/marriage (*Lk 24: 44-53*)

-- Trust God to right every wrong for you. How?

- Let God change your heart, mind, and vision to align with the Word of God.

- *Claim His promises* (Make a list of His biblical promises and speak them over your spouse and family daily. Start with Ps 91)

- *Obey His commandments.* (Make a list of His commandments)

More For Separated/Divorce Couples:

Reassess Your Issues & Forgive

When did the relationship start falling apart?

_____
_____
_____
_____
_____
_____

What was your part in it?

_____
_____
_____
_____
_____
_____

Where is a good starting point to start the forgiveness process?

*Hint - start with the small things.

_____
_____

_____

_____

_____

How can you both come to an agreement to truly forgive and promise not bring up each other's past transgressions?

_____

_____

_____

_____

Find scriptures in the Bible that you all can begin to stand on. Speak them to each other every day until they sink in to your hearts.

* Realign Yourself and Your Lives To God and His Word

-- *Commit those scriptures to memory* that you and your spouse agreed to stand on.

-- Pray to God together

-- Study His Word daily

-- Find a church home

-- *Find married Christians that you can meet and talk with regularly* about issues arising in the marriage. Stop it early before it catches fire and becomes a bigger issue.

-- *Set rules for arguments* before an argument and do not break them

-- Do not go to bed angry. EVER!

* ReCommit To Loving God and Your Spouse Like Never Before!

-- Begin to *love your spouse like Christ loved you* when you were your "old self."

-- Make an irrevocable date night every week that cannot be broken for six months

-- Spend no less than one hour a day praying by yourself, then together, worshiping God, and studying your Bible. (If you have kids, have them join in. The word says, *"Train up a child in the way they should go, and when they are old, it will not depart from them (Prv 22:6).* You are the parent. They follow you, not the other way around.

-- *Do not get any advice about your relationship from your family, friends, etc....* Inquire of the Lord and he will show you and tell you all you need to know.

-- *Make your marriage your first ministry.* Build your life around God and it, not vice versa.

~APPENDIX B~

Daily Devotional:

-- A Letter To Me From The Lord:

This letter came from the Lord for such a time as this. God wants you to know this. I have written many versions of this for bible studies, friends, etc. So please let it speak directly to you and minister to your heart.

Insert your name wherever you see mine.

Dear _____,

I know everything about you. Psalm 139:1

I know when you sit down and when you rise up. Psalm: 139:2.

I am familiar with all your ways. Psalm: 139:3

For I knew you before I put you into your mother's womb. Jer:1:45

I made you in my likeness. Gen:1:27

You are fearfully and wonderfully made. Psalm 139:14

I am not distant nor am I angry, but I am the complete expression of Love. 1John 4:16

It is my desire to lavish my love on you because I love you with an everlasting love. 1 John 3:1

My plan for your future has always been filled with hope. Jer 29:11.

My thoughts toward you are countless as the sand on the seashores Ps 139:17-18

I rejoice over you with singing. Zeph 3:17

I will never stop doing good to you. Jer 32:40

You, Wendy Darline, are my treasured possession. Exodus 19:5

I desire to establish you with all my heart and all my soul. Jer 32:41

I want to show you great and marvelous things. Jer 33:3

Delight yourself in me and I will give you the desires of your heart. Ps 37:4

Because I gave these desires to you. Phill 2:13

I am able to do more for you than you could possibly imagine. Eph 3:20

For I am your Great Encourager 2Thes 2:16-17.

I am also your father who comforts you in all your troubles. 2 Cor 1:

When you are brokenhearted, I will be close to you. Psalms 34:18.

I will never leave you or forsake you. Deut 31:6

I will wipe away every tear from your eyes. Rev 21:3-4

I will take away all pain you have suffered here on this earth. Rev 21:3-4

Because I am your Father, and I love you even as I love my son Jesus. Jn 17:23

Jesus is my love for you revealed in the flesh. John 17:26

He came to show you that I am for you not against you. Romans 8:31

I tell you that I am not counting your sins. 2 Cor 5:18-19

I gave up everything I loved so that I might gain your love. Rom 8:31-32

Nothing will ever separate you from my Love again. Rom 8:38-39

Come here to me, watch and see how I will vindicate you. Rom 12:19

I will give you rest. MT 11:28-29

I will restore you. Joel 2:25

I will restore your health, and heal all your wounds. Jer 30:17

I have anointed you. Luke 4:18, Is 61:1.

You are the splendor of Me, your King. Strengthened with power through my spirit. Eph 3:16-19

I created you to be a beautiful crown from among all the ash! Is 61:3b

Take this oil of gladness that I have made and prepare yourself to be a bride. Is 61:3

Love your father, God

-- Prayer For Patience In God's Timing:

Glorious Father,

Your ways are not my ways; your time is not my time, so I will trust in you and lean not on my own understanding, but in all things I will request wisdom. Thank you for the mind of Christ. In Jesus' Mighty Name, Amen and Amen

-- Prayer To Break The Lone Ranger Spirit Off Of You:

Dear Father in Heaven,

Forgive me of all of my sins. Father, I forgive those who have hurt or sinned against me and caused me to come into agreement with the spirit of self-reliance and self-preservation. I pull that root up and all other roots attached to it (such as selfishness, callousness, narcissism) right now in Jesus name and I cancel those hurts and ask that Your love come into those hurt places in my heart and heal my brokenness. Holy Spirit, convict me from this moment forward if that lone ranger spirit rises anywhere within me. Lord I now ask that anyone I hurt in the process of being self-reliant, anyone that I may have hurt, neglected or rejected because of that spirit of lone ranger, I ask that you heal their hearts and give me an opportunity to make it right with them. *Thank you for hearing my prayers. Thank you for keeping me in times when I didn't deserve it. You are the God of Heaven and Earth. You are the Holy Redeemer and the Healer of Broken Hearts. I am healed. I am delivered. I am sanctified by the blood of Jesus. In Jesus name, Amen*

Now go make two lists: one for the people who hurt you and another for the ones who have been hurt by you. Forgive those who hurt you and pray for God to bless them. Now take the list of the ones who were hurt by you. Pray for each one of them. Call them if you're able to. If you're not able to, write a letter to them. Go with a contrite heart and realize you hurt them. So if they won't talk to you, that's fine. But you have to make the first move and God will do the rest.

-- Prayer To Break Soul Ties:

* Make a list of everybody you fornicated with (had sex with outside of marriage)
* Once you have the list, say this:

Lord God,

I ask for your forgiveness for fornicating outside of marriage. It is a sin against you, Jesus and the Holy Spirit. I will honor your commands, laws, and precepts and treat my body like the temple of the Holy Spirit that it is. (Say your name) I forgive you. I know better, and I will do better.

In Jesus' Name, Amen!

* Next, say these words after each name:

Lord, I ask that you forgive me for creating an unhealthy soul tie with (person's name). I give them back to you and ask that you would cancel the soul tie. Forgive me of any offense, sin, or lie that I committed against them. I ask that you make them whole, bless them and help them find the perfect mate you created for them. In Jesus' Name, Amen

-- Call To Salvation Prayer:

Lord God,

I want you in my life. I need to know you. I need a relationship with you. Be my Lord. Be my savior. Forgive me for all of my sins. Thank you for sending your only begotten son, Jesus Christ, to die on the cross for me and resurrecting him. From this day forward, Jesus Christ is the Lord of my life. Forever and ever. Amen.

-- Call To Dedicate Your Marriage to God:

My Lord & God,

Thank you for hearing our prayers. Forgive us for not seeking you diligently day in and day out. We have let the issues of the world interrupt and steal our time together. We repent wholeheartedly for putting anything before You. We choose from this moment forward to make You the most important person in our life and to cherish our time together. We will include You in all of my decision-making. We will move when Your Spirit of Power comes upon us and not hesitate.. We believe in You. We want You and need You as the anchor in our life. All praise, glory, and honor to You, The Most High God in all things.
In Jesus' Majestic Name, Amen.

-- Prayer For Alignment/Realignment With God
Dear Abba,

I am checking in with you. May my footsteps be in perfect alignment with your will for my life right now. Please reveal to me anything, anyone, or any situation that displeases you so that I can remove it. Anything that you did not call me to do I lay it down at the altar right now. I thank you, Lord in advance for your perfect timing, your faithfulness and patience with me to make sure that I finish my race successfully. In Jesus' Marvelous Name, Amen

~ INDEX ~

Romans 8:

Present Suffering and Future Glory

Therefore, there is now no condemnation for those who are in Christ Jesus, 2 because through Christ Jesus the law of the Spirit who gives life has set you[a] free from the law of sin and death. 3 For what the law was powerless to do because it was weakened by the flesh,[b] God did by sending his own Son in the likeness of sinful flesh to be a sin offering.[c]And so he condemned sin in the flesh, 4 in order that the righteous requirement of the law might be fully met in us, who do not live according to the flesh but according to the Spirit. 5 Those who live according to the flesh have their minds set on what the flesh desires; but those who live in accordance with the Spirit have their minds set on what the Spirit desires. 6 The mind governed by the flesh is death, but the mind governed by the Spirit is life and peace. 7 The mind governed by the flesh is hostile to God; it does not submit to God's law, nor can it do so. 8 Those who are in the realm of the flesh cannot please God. 9 You, however, are not in the realm of the flesh but are in the realm of the Spirit, if indeed the Spirit of God lives in you. And if anyone does not have the Spirit of Christ, they do not belong to Christ. 10 But if Christ is in you, then even though your body is subject to death because of sin, the Spirit gives life[d] because of righteousness. 11 And if the Spirit of him who raised Jesus from the dead is living in you, he who raised Christ from the dead will also give life to your mortal bodies because of[e] his Spirit who lives in you. 12 Therefore, brothers and sisters, we have an obligation—but it is not to the flesh, to live according to it. 13 For if you live according to the flesh, you will die; but if by the Spirit you put to death the misdeeds of the body, you will live. 14 For those who are led by the Spirit of God are the children of God. 15 The Spirit you received does not make you slaves, so that you live in fear again; rather, the Spirit you received brought about your adoption to sonship.[f] And by him we cry, "Abba,[g] Father." 16 The Spirit himself testifies with our spirit that we are God's children. 17 Now if we are children, then we are heirs—heirs of God and co-heirs with Christ, if indeed we share in his sufferings in order that we may also share in his glory. 18 I consider that our present sufferings are not worth comparing with the glory that will be revealed in us. 19 For the creation waits in eager expectation for the children of God to be revealed. 20 For the creation was subjected to frustration, not by its own choice, but by the will of the one who subjected it, in hope 21 that[h] the creation itself will be liberated from its bondage to decay and brought into the freedom and glory of the children of God. 22 We know that the whole creation has been groaning as in the pains of childbirth right up to the present time. 23 Not only so, but we ourselves, who have the firstfruits of the Spirit, groan inwardly as we wait eagerly for our adoption to sonship, the redemption of our bodies. 24 For in this hope we were saved. But hope that is seen is no hope at all. Who hopes for what they already have? 25 But if we hope for what we do not yet have, we wait for it patiently. 26 In the same way, the Spirit helps us in our weakness. We do not know what we ought to pray for, but the Spirit himself intercedes for us through wordless groans. 27 And he who searches our hearts knows the mind of the Spirit, 28 And we know that in all things God works for the good of those who love him, who[i] have been called according to his purpose. 29 For those God foreknew he also predestined to be conformed to the image of his Son, that he might be the firstborn among many brothers and sisters.30 And those he predestined, he also called; those he called, he also justified; those he justified, he also glorified. 31 What, then, shall we say in response to these things? If God is for us, who can be against us? 32 He who did not spare his own Son, but gave him up for us all—how will he not also, along with him, graciously give us all things? 33 Who will bring any charge against those whom God has chosen? It is God who justifies. 34 Who then is the one who condemns? No one. Christ Jesus who died—more than that, who was raised to life—is at the right hand of God and is also interceding for us. 35 Who shall separate us from the love of Christ? Shall trouble or hardship or persecution or famine or nakedness or danger or sword? 36 As it is written: "For your sake we face death all day long; we are considered as sheep to be slaughtered."[j] 37 No, in all these things we are more than conquerors through him who loved us. 38 For I am convinced that neither death nor life, neither angels nor demons,[k] neither the present nor the future, nor any powers, 39 neither height nor depth, nor anything else in all creation, will be able to separate us from the love of God that is in Christ Jesus our Lord.

Proverbs 31: 10b-31 The Wife of Noble Character:

'10 [b]A wife of noble character who can find? She is worth far more than rubies. 11 Her husband has full confidence in her and lacks nothing of value. 12 She brings him good, not harm, all the days of her life. 13 She selects wool and flax and works with eager hands. 14 She is like the merchant ships, bringing her food from afar. 15 She gets up while it is still night; she provides food for her family and portions for her female servants. 16 She considers a field and buys it; out of her earnings she plants a vineyard. 17 She sets about her work vigorously; her arms are strong for her tasks. 18 She sees that her trading is profitable, and her lamp does not go out at night. 19 In her hand she holds the distaff and grasps the spindle with her fingers. 20 She opens her arms to the poor and extends her hands to the needy. 21 When it snows, she has no fear for her household; for all of them are clothed in scarlet. 22 She makes coverings for her bed; she is clothed in fine linen and purple. 23 Her husband is respected at the city gate, where he takes his seat among the elders of the land. 24 She makes linen garments and sells them, and supplies the merchants with sashes. 25 She is clothed with strength and dignity; she can laugh at the days to come. 26 She speaks with wisdom, and faithful instruction is on her tongue. 27 She watches over the affairs of her household and does not eat the bread of idleness. 28 Her children arise and call her blessed; her husband also, and he praises her: 29 "Many women do noble things, but you surpass them all." 30 Charm is deceptive, and beauty is fleeting; but a woman who fears the Lord is to be praised. 31 Honor her for all that her hands have done, and let her works bring her praise at the city gate.'

Isaiah. 61:

"The Spirit of the Lord God is upon me; because the Lord hath anointed me to preach good tidings unto the meek; he hath sent me to bind up the brokenhearted, to proclaim liberty to the captives, and the opening of the prison to them that are bound; 2 To proclaim the acceptable year of the Lord, and the day of vengeance of our God; to comfort all that mourn; 3 To appoint unto them that mourn in Zion, to give unto them beauty for ashes, the oil of joy for mourning, the garment of praise for the spirit of heaviness; that they might be called trees of righteousness, the planting of the Lord, that he might be glorified. 4 And they shall build the old wastes, they shall raise up the former desolations, and they shall repair the waste cities, the desolations of many generations. 5 And strangers shall stand and feed your flocks, and the sons of the alien shall be your plowmen and your vinedressers. 6 But ye shall be named the Priests of the Lord: men shall call you the Ministers of our God: ye shall eat the riches of the Gentiles, and in their glory shall ye boast yourselves. 7 For your shame ye shall have double; and for confusion they shall rejoice in their portion: therefore in their land they shall possess the double: everlasting joy shall be unto them. 8 For I the Lord love judgment, I hate robbery for burnt offering; and I will direct their work in truth, and I will make an everlasting covenant with them. 9 And their seed shall be known among the Gentiles, and their offspring among the people: all that see them shall acknowledge them, that they are the seed which the Lord hath blessed. 10 I will greatly rejoice in the Lord, my soul shall be joyful in my God; for he hath clothed me with the garments of salvation, he hath covered me with the robe of righteousness, as a bridegroom decketh himself with ornaments, and as a bride adorned herself with her jewels. 11 For as the earth bringeth forth her bud, and as the garden causeth the things that are sown in it to spring forth; so the Lord God will cause righteousness and praise to spring forth before all the nations."

Ruth 4:1-17:

"Then went Boaz up to the gate, and sat him down there: and, behold, the kinsman of whom Boaz spake came by; unto whom he said, Ho, such a one! turn aside, sit down here. And he turned aside, and sat down. 2 And he took ten men of the elders of the city, and said, Sit ye down here. And they sat down. 3 And he said unto the kinsman, Naomi, that is come again out of the country of Moab, selleth a parcel of land, which was our brother Elimelech's: 4 And I thought to advertise thee, saying, Buy it before the inhabitants, and before the elders of my people. If thou wilt redeem it, redeem it: but if thou wilt not redeem it, then tell me, that I may know: for there is none to redeem it beside thee; and I am after thee. And he said, I will redeem it. 5 Then said Boaz, What day thou buyest the field of the hand of Naomi, thou must buy it also of Ruth the Moabitess, the wife of the dead, to raise up the name of the dead upon his inheritance. 6 And the kinsman said, I cannot redeem it for myself, lest I mar mine own inheritance: redeem thou my right to thyself; for I cannot redeem it. 7 Now this was the manner in former time in Israel concerning redeeming and concerning changing, for to confirm all things; a man plucked off his shoe, and gave it to his neighbour: and this was a testimony in Israel. 8 Therefore the kinsman said unto Boaz, Buy it for thee. So he drew off his shoe. 9 And Boaz said unto the elders, and unto all the people, Ye are witnesses this day, that I have bought all that was Elimelech's, and all that was Chilion's and Mahlon's, of the hand of Naomi. 10 Moreover Ruth the Moabitess, the wife of Mahlon, have I purchased to be my wife, to raise up the name of the dead upon his inheritance, that the name of the dead be not cut off from among his brethren, and from the gate of his place: ye are witnesses this day. 11 And all the people that were in the gate, and the elders, said, We are witnesses. The Lord make the woman that is come into thine house like Rachel and like Leah, which two did build the house of Israel: and do thou worthily in Ephratah, and be famous in Bethlehem: 12 And let thy house be like the house of Pharez, whom Tamar bare unto Judah, of the seed which the Lord shall give thee of this young woman. 13 So Boaz took Ruth, and she was his wife: and when he went in unto her, the Lord gave her conception, and she bare a son. 14 And the women said unto Naomi, Blessed be the Lord, which hath not left thee this day without a kinsman, that his name may be famous in Israel. 15 And he shall be unto thee a restorer of thy life, and a nourisher of thine old age: for thy daughter in law, which loveth thee, which is better to thee than seven sons, hath born him. 16 And Naomi took the child, and laid it in her bosom, and became nurse unto it. 17 And the women her neighbours gave it a name, saying, There is a son born to Naomi; they called his name Obed: the father of Jesse, the father of David."

1 Kings 19:

"And Ahab told Jezebel all that Elijah had done, and withal how he had slain all the prophets with the sword. 2 Then Jezebel sent a messenger unto Elijah, saying, So let the gods do to me, and more also, if I make not thy life as the life of one of them by tomorrow about this time. 3 And when he saw that, he arose, and went for his life, and came to Beersheba, which belongeth to Judah, and left his servant there. 4 But he himself went a day's journey into the wilderness, and came and sat down under a juniper tree: and he requested for himself that he might die; and said, It is enough; now, O Lord, take away my life; for I am not better than my fathers. 5 And as he lay and slept under a juniper tree, behold, then an angel touched him, and said unto him, Arise and eat. 6 And he looked, and, behold, there was a cake baken on the coals, and a cruse of water at his head. And he did eat and drink, and laid him down again. 7 And the angel of the Lord came again the second time, and touched him, and said, Arise and eat; because the journey is too great for thee. 8 And he arose, and did eat and drink, and went in the strength of that meat forty days and forty nights unto Horeb the mount of God. 9 And he came thither unto a cave, and lodged there; and, behold, the word of the Lord came to him, and he said unto him, What doest thou here, Elijah? 10 And he said, I have been very jealous for the Lord God of hosts: for the children of Israel have forsaken thy covenant, thrown down thine altars, and slain thy prophets with the sword; and I, even I only, am left; and they seek my life, to take it away. 11 And he said, Go forth, and stand upon the mount before the Lord. And, behold, the Lord passed by, and a great and strong wind rent the mountains, and brake in pieces the rocks before the Lord; but the Lord Was not in the wind: and after the wind an earthquake; but the Lord was not in the earthquake: 12 And after the earthquake a fire; but the Lord was not in the fire: and after the fire a still small voice. 13 And it was so, when Elijah heard it, that he wrapped his face in his mantle, and went out, and stood in the entering in of the cave. And, behold, there came a voice unto him, and said, What doest thou here, Elijah? 14 And he said, I have been very jealous for the Lord God of hosts: because the children of Israel have forsaken thy covenant, thrown down thine altars, and slain thy prophets with the sword; and I, even I only, am left; and they seek my life, to take it away. 15 And the Lord said unto him, Go, return on thy way to the wilderness of Damascus: and when thou comest, anoint Hazael to be king over Syria: 16 And Jehu the son of Nimshi shalt thou anoint to be king over Israel: and Elisha the son of Shaphat of

Abelmeholah shalt thou anoint to be prophet in thy room. 17 And it shall come to pass, that him that escapeth the sword of Hazael shall Jehu slay: and him that escapeth from the sword of Jehu shall Elisha slay. 18 Yet I have left me seven thousand in Israel, all the knees which have not bowed unto Baal, and every mouth which hath not kissed him. 19 So he departed thence, and found Elisha the son of Shaphat, who was plowing with twelve yoke of oxen before him, and he with the twelfth: and Elijah passed by him, and cast his mantle upon him. 20 And he left the oxen, and ran after Elijah, and said, Let me, I pray thee, kiss my father and my mother, and then I will follow thee. And he said unto him, Go back again: for what have I done to thee? 21 And he returned back from him, and took a yoke of oxen, and slew them, and boiled their flesh with the instruments of the oxen, and gave unto the people, and they did eat. Then he arose, and went after Elijah, and ministered unto him."

1 Sam 25: Death of Samuel (Abigail)

"Then Samuel died; and the Israelites gathered together and lamented for him, and buried him at his home in Ramah. And David arose and went down to the Wilderness of Paran.[a}

2 Now there was a man in Maon whose business was in Carmel, and the man was very rich. He had three thousand sheep and a thousand goats. And he was shearing his sheep in Carmel. 3 The name of the man was Nabal, and the name of his wife Abigail. And she was a woman of good understanding and beautiful appearance; but the man was harsh and evil in his doings. He was of the house of Caleb. 4 When David heard in the wilderness that Nabal was shearing his sheep, 5 David sent ten young men; and David said to the young men, "Go up to Carmel, go to Nabal, and greet him in my name. 6 And thus you shall say to him who lives in prosperity: 'Peace be to you, peace to your house, and peace to all that you have! 7 Now I have heard that you have shearers. Your shepherds were with us, and we did not hurt them, nor was there anything missing from them all the while they were in Carmel. 8 Ask your young men, and they will tell you. Therefore let my young men find favor in your eyes, for we come on a feast day. Please give whatever comes to your hand to your servants and to your son David.'" 9 So when David's young men came, they spoke to Nabal according to all these words in the name of David, and waited. 10 Then Nabal answered David's servants, and said, "Who is David, and who is the son of Jesse? There are many servants nowadays who break away each one from his

master. 11 Shall I then take my bread and my water and my meat that I have killed for my shearers, and give it to men when I do not know where they are from?" 12 So David's young men turned on their heels and went back; and they came and told him all these words. 13 Then David said to his men, "Every man gird on his sword." So every man girded on his sword, and David also girded on his sword. And about four hundred men went with David, and two hundred stayed with the supplies. 14 Now one of the young men told Abigail, Nabal's wife, saying, "Look, David sent messengers from the wilderness to greet our master; and he reviled them. 15 But the men were very good to us, and we were not hurt, nor did we miss anything as long as we accompanied them, when we were in the fields. 16 They were a wall to us both by night and day, all the time we were with them keeping the sheep. 17 Now therefore, know and consider what you will do, for harm is determined against our master and against all his household. For he is such a scoundrel[b] that one cannot speak to him." 18 Then Abigail made haste and took two hundred loaves of bread, two skins of wine, five sheep already dressed, five seahs of roasted grain,one hundred clusters of raisins, and two hundred cakes of figs, and loaded them on donkeys. 19 And she said to her servants, "Go on before me; see, I am coming after you." But she did not tell her husband Nabal. 20 So it was, as she rode on the donkey, that she went down under cover of the hill; and there were David and his men, coming down toward her, and she met them. 21 Now David had said, "Surely in vain I have protected all that this fellow has in the wilderness, so that nothing was missed of all that belongs to him. And he has repaid me evil for good. 22 May God do so, and more also, to the enemies of David, if I leave one male of all who belong to him by morning light." 23 Now when Abigail saw David, she dismounted quickly from the donkey, fell on her face before David, and bowed down to the ground. 24 So she fell at his feet and said: "On me, my lord, on me let this iniquity be! And please let your maidservant speak in your ears, and hear the words of your maidservant. 25 Please, let not my lord regard this scoundrel Nabal. For as his name is, so is he: Nabal[c] is his name, and folly is with him! But I, your maidservant, did not see the young men of my lord whom you sent. 26 Now therefore, my lord, as the Lord lives and as your soul lives, since the Lord has held you back from coming to bloodshed and from avenging yourself with your own hand, now then, let your enemies and those who seek harm for my lord be as Nabal. 27 And now this present which your maidservant has brought to my lord, let it be given to the young men who follow my lord. 28 Please forgive the trespass of your maidservant. For the Lord will certainly make for my lord an enduring house, because my lord fights the battles of the Lord, and evil is not found in you throughout your days. 29 Yet a man has risen to pursue you and seek your life, but the life of my lord shall be bound in the bundle of the living with the Lord your God; and the lives of your enemies He shall sling out, as from the pocket of a sling. 30 And it shall come to pass, when the Lord has done for my lord according to all the good that He has spoken concerning you, and has appointed you ruler over Israel, 31 that this will be no grief to you, nor offense of heart to my lord, either that you have shed blood without cause, or that my lord has avenged himself. But when the Lord has dealt well with my lord, then remember your maidservant." 32 Then David said to Abigail:

"Blessed is the Lord God of Israel, who sent you this day to meet me! 33 And blessed is your advice and blessed are you, because you have kept me this day from coming to bloodshed and from avenging myself with my own hand. 34 For indeed, as the Lord God of Israel lives, who has kept me back from hurting you, unless you had hurried and come to meet me, surely by morning light no males would have been left to Nabal!" 35 So David received from her hand what she had brought him, and said to her, "Go up in peace to your house. See, I have heeded your voice and respected your person." 36 Now Abigail went to Nabal, and there he was, holding a feast in his house, like the feast of a king. And Nabal's heart was merry within him, for he was very drunk; therefore she told him nothing, little or much, until morning light. 37 So it was, in the morning, when the wine had gone from Nabal, and his wife had told him these things, that his heart died within him, and he became like a stone. 38 Then it happened, after about ten days, that the Lord struck Nabal, and he died. 39 So when David heard that Nabal was dead, he said, "Blessed be the Lord, who has pleaded the cause of my reproach from the hand of Nabal, and has kept His servant from evil! For the Lord has returned the wickedness of Nabal on his own head." And David sent and proposed to Abigail, to take her as his wife. 40 When the servants of David had come to Abigail at Carmel, they spoke to her saying, "David sent us to you, to ask you to become his wife." 41 Then she arose, bowed her face to the earth, and said, "Here is your maidservant, a servant to wash the feet of the servants of my lord." 42 So Abigail rose in haste and rode on a donkey, attended by five of her maidens; and she followed the messengers of David, and became his wife. 43 David also took Ahinoam of Jezreel, and so both of them were his wives."

Luke 10:28-33 28:

"... For which of you, intending to build a tower, sitteth not down first, and counteth the cost, whether he have sufficient to finish it? 29 Lest haply, after he hath laid the foundation, and is not able to finish it, all that behold it begin to mock him, 30 Saying, This man began to build, and was not able to finish. 31 Or what king, going to make war against another king, sitteth not down first, and consulted whether he be able with ten thousand to meet him that cometh against him with twenty thousand? 32 Or else, while the other is yet a great way off, he sendeth an ambassage, and desireth conditions of peace. 33 So likewise, whosoever he be of you that forsaketh not all that he hath, he cannot be my disciple.

Mt 25: 1-13:

Then shall the kingdom of heaven be likened unto ten virgins, which took their lamps, and went forth to meet the bridegroom. 2 And five of them were wise, and five were foolish. 3 They that were foolish took their lamps, and took no oil with them: 4 But the wise took oil in their vessels with their lamps. 5 While the bridegroom tarried, they all slumbered and slept. 6 And at midnight there was a cry made, Behold, the bridegroom cometh; go ye out to meet him. 7 Then all those virgins arose, and trimmed their lamps. 8 And the foolish said unto the wise, Give us of your oil; for our lamps are gone out. 9 But the wise answered, saying, Not so; lest there be not enough for us and you: but go ye rather to them that sell, and buy for yourselves. 10 And while they went to buy, the bridegroom came; and they that were ready went in with him to the marriage: and the door was shut. 11 Afterward came also the other virgins, saying, Lord, Lord, open to us. 12 But he answered and said, Verily I say unto you, I know you not. 13 Watch therefore, for ye know neither the day nor the hour wherein the Son of man cometh.

1 Corinthians 7 (NKJV):

Principles of Marriage
7 Now concerning the things of which you wrote to me: It is good for a man not to touch a woman. 2 Nevertheless, because of sexual immorality, let each man have his own wife, and let each woman

have her own husband. 3 Let the husband render to his wife the affection due her, and likewise also the wife to her husband. 4 The wife does not have authority over her own body, but the husband does. And likewise the husband does not have authority over his own body, but the wife does. 5 Do not deprive one another except with consent for a time, that you may give yourselves to fasting and prayer; and come together again so that Satan does not tempt you because of your lack of self-control. 6 But I say this as a concession, not as a commandment. 7 For I wish that all men were even as I myself. But each one has his own gift from God, one in this manner and another in that. 8 But I say to the unmarried and to the widows: It is good for them if they remain even as I am; 9 but if they cannot exercise self-control, let them marry. For it is better to marry than to burn with passion.

-- Keep Your Marriage Vows

10 Now to the married I command, yet not I but the Lord: A wife is not to depart from her husband. 11 But even if she does depart, let her remain unmarried or be reconciled to her husband. And a husband is not to divorce his wife. 12 But to the rest I, not the Lord, say: If any brother has a wife who does not believe, and she is willing to live with him, let him not divorce her. 13 And a woman who has a husband who does not believe, if he is willing to live

with her, let her not divorce him. 14 For the unbelieving husband is sanctified by the wife, and the unbelieving wife is sanctified by the husband; otherwise your children would be unclean, but now they are holy. 15 But if the unbeliever departs, let him depart; a brother or a sister is not under bondage in such cases. But God has called us to peace. 16 For how do you know, O wife, whether you will save your husband? Or how do you know, O husband, whether you will save your wife?

-- Live as You Are Called

17 But as God has distributed to each one, as the Lord has called each one, so let him walk. And so I ordain in all the churches. 18 Was anyone called while circumcised? Let him not become uncircumcised. Was anyone called while uncircumcised? Let him not be circumcised. 19 Circumcision is nothing and uncircumcision is nothing, but keeping the commandments of God is what matters. 20 Let each one remain in the same calling in which he was called. 21 Were you called while a slave? Do not be concerned about it; but if you can be made free, rather use it. 22 For he who is called in the Lord while a slave is the Lord's freedman. Likewise he who is called while free is Christ's slave. 23 You were bought at a price; do not become slaves of men. 24 Brethren, let each one remain with God in that state in

which he was called."

Prv 6:16-19:

"These six things the Lord hates,

Yes, seven are an abomination to Him:

¹⁷ A proud look,

A lying tongue,

Hands that shed innocent blood,

¹⁸ A heart that devises wicked plans,

Feet that are swift in running to evil,

¹⁹ A false witness who speaks lies,

And one who sows discord among brethren"

Gen 22:1-19:

1Some time later God tested Abraham. He said to him, "Abraham!" "Here I am," he replied. 2 Then God said, "Take your son, your only son, whom you love—Isaac—and go to the region of Moriah. Sacrifice him there as a burnt offering on a mountain I will show you." 3 Early the next morning Abraham got up and loaded his donkey. He took with him two of his servants and his son Isaac. When he had cut enough wood for the burnt offering, he set out for the place God had told him about. 4 On the third day Abraham looked up and saw the place in the distance. 5 He said to his servants, "Stay here with the donkey while I and the boy go over there. We will worship and then we will come back to you." 6 Abraham took the wood for the burnt offering and placed it on his son Isaac, and he himself carried the fire and the knife. As the two of them went on together, 7 Isaac spoke up and said to his father Abraham, "Father?" "Yes, my son?" Abraham replied. "The fire and wood are here," Isaac said, "but where is the lamb for the burnt offering?" 8 Abraham answered, "God himself will provide the lamb for the burnt offering, my son." And the two of them went on together. 9 When they reached the place God had told him about, Abraham built an altar there and arranged the wood on it. He bound his son Isaac and laid him on the altar, on top of the wood. 10 Then he reached out his hand and took the knife to slay his son. 11 But the angel of the Lord called out to him from heaven, "Abraham! Abraham!" "Here I am," he replied. 12 "Do not lay a hand on the boy," he said. "Do not do anything to him. Now I know that you fear God, because you have not withheld from me your son, your only son." 13 Abraham looked up and there in a thicket he saw a ram[a] caught by its horns. He went over and took the ram and sacrificed it as a burnt offering instead of his son. 14 So

Abraham called that place The Lord Will Provide. And to this day it is said, "On the mountain of the Lord it will be provided." 15 The angel of the Lord called to Abraham from heaven a second time16 and said, "I swear by myself, declares the Lord, that because you have done this and have not withheld your son, your only son, 17 I will surely bless you and make your descendants as numerous as the stars in the sky and as the sand on the seashore. Your descendants will take possession of the cities of their enemies, 18 and through your offspring[b]all nations on earth will be blessed,[c] because you have obeyed me." 19 Then Abraham returned to his servants, and they set off together for Beersheba. And Abraham stayed in Beersheba."

You were not created to be alone.

You were not created to be with just anyone.

You need your God-mate.

Wait for your God-mate.

Satan prowls around like a roaring lion seeking whose marriage he can steal, kill, destroy and devour. We don't wan t it to be our marriage, and we especially don't want it to be yours. Please join us in praying daily for the healing of marriages around the world. God loves his church. Jesus loves his bride. Now it's time to love our spouses the way God intended and Jesus demonstrated.

Amen

Thank you for taking the time to read our story and allowing us to be transparent and raw with all of you.

We pray this book inspires you, heals you and sets you on your God path, in Jesus mighty name.

God Bless,

Eric. and Wendy Darline. Ingram

Co-Authors, Helpmates, and Children of Almighty God

www.ingramcontent.com/pod-product-compliance
Lightning Source LLC
LaVergne TN
LVHW041608070426
835507LV00008B/173